Islam versus the Rest: World on the Brink of Disaster

Author: Shabbir H M Tankiwala

Author All Rights Reserved

It is not just a requirement but necessary to have a roof over our head, a dream of each one of us to have a house of our own, we humans are the only species living on this Planet (Earth) who needs to pay taxes, we humans have developed such a system that we need to work to earn money to have food on the table, we need to pay our monthly bills.

Power of money; arguably the most desired power that every living person in this world dreams of possessing it, wealth and money have immense strength and those fortunate people who have it, they relish every moment of their life.

Uncertain times are becoming even more uncertain, these are challenging moments for the entire humanity, sort out one problem and another problem rushes in, too many challenges but too few resources available to solve ever existing difficult problems and for dealing with incredibly difficult challenges.

Far too many challenges before us, so many problems, despite so many remarkably intelligent and well-judging minds, yet difficult to find solutions for most of the problems we humans are burdened with.

Social problems, healthcare related problems, widespread religious and racial discrimination, ecological imbalance and climatic problems, demographic problems, so many problems and challenges, but, who are responsible for all these excruciating problems?

Rising religious intolerance and hatred crimes, steady increase in domestic violence and workplace violence, sharp increase in cases of sexual harassments, forced marriages, forced prostitutions and gruesome incidents of honour killings, women and children particularly vulnerable.

Religious extremism and terrorism is menacing we all know and we all are worried about, but, some studies and surveys have discovered that Climatic and weather related problems are unquestionably responsible for increase spread of diseases, and for rising poverty and hunger in our world, frequent natural disasters have displaced and have made millions of people homeless in many different countries around the world.

These are nerve-wrecking viciously chaotic moments for the entire humanity, unprecedented difficult challenges, Religious wars, substantial rise in extremism and terrorism, racial and religious intolerance sparking hatred crimes, vulnerable people are being discriminated, nepotism, favouritism and corruption in high places, religious prejudice and cognitive bias less-talented and underserving people are progressing and prospering while much more talented and deserving people are being ignored and disregarded, dwindling job and professional opportunities, rising unemployment, declining productivity and to make matter worse increase global warming, weather and climate problems.

Crisis is either created by man or crisis is created by nature.

"**Arab Spring revolutionary movement**" that has or had not only turned into nightmare for the Arabs but for the Europeans and Americans as well. "**Arab spring**" is the name given by the western media to the Revolutionary Movement, a struggle that started in the year 2011 by the beleaguered and long suppressed Arab citizens to seek civil-rights and better quality of life and freedom of speech, demanding democracy and accountability, the protest demonstrations for freedom from their respective country's ruling dictatorial regimes that first started in a small town in **Tunisia** soon spread to many west-Asian and North-African Muslim dominated countries. But, what seemingly started in earnest as a sincere peaceful movement to seek democratic rights in which both men and women equally participated to demonstrate against the authoritarian and dictatorial regimes in countries like Libya, Egypt, Yemen and Tunisia etc, but, no sooner had the struggle started. The whole purpose of revolutionary movement was crushed by the opportunists Islamists jihadi forces and it was twisted and turned into full blown communal and sectarian conflict, deliberately taking advantage of generation old divide between Shia and Sunni, Sunni and Kurdish and bitter rivalry amongst various other religious and ethnic communities in Islamic world, many alleged state sponsored and supported groups of extremist Islamic fundamentalist forces have started unrelenting and unending **Religious wars** which have destabilized not just the entire Arabian region but also the whole world.

The Salafists and militants belonging to Sunni-Muslim fundamentalist jihadi (holy-warriors) groups systematically turned the Arab spring movement into full fledge sectarian and communal conflict, to achieve their selfish objective the Sunni-Muslim jihadist groups like the most notorious amongst them "ISIS, Al-Qaeda, Al-Nusra, Al Shabaab and Boko Haram," started to terrorise people and caused havoc and fear in the civil society, the monstrous jihadi elements brutally started enforcing their draconian diktats, forcing upon extreme hard-core Islamic religious Sharia law on common people.

Particularly hard pressed are/were the women belonging to almost every religious and ethnic communities and racial groups, The Islamic militants brutally intimidate people belonging to all the Non Sunni Muslim communities, and even the followers of Sunni-Islam especially those people who are liberal and secular are not spared, the Islamists jihadists or to say the 'Muslim terrorists' terrorizes even the Sunni-Muslim folks who are secular and liberal, the jihadists threatens them of dire consequences if they do not follow the Islamic sharia law and abide by it, these jihadist groups have not hesitated even in raping and killing Sunni-Muslims those who dare or dared to oppose their diktat.

Islamic religious wars and sectarian conflicts in the west-Asia and N-Africa the Islamic militants have reserved their harsh brutality for non-Sunni Muslims, they are savage and callous when it comes to dealing with people belonging to communities such as the "Shias, Christians, Kurdish, Jewish, Yazidis etc," the various Sunni-Muslim jihadists and terrorist groups vigorously loots wealth, ferociously rapes women and mercilessly kills men.

Dispute over territories, the political, religious and ideological differences in Islamic countries. The war of ideologies in Muslim dominated west-Asia and north-African countries, sharp differences over religious and cultural issues, rivalries and distrust persist among Muslims. The social and political problems that viciously started in 2011 in several Islamic countries in W-Asia and N-Africa, many prominent Islamic countries brutally harmed, among the worst affected by sectarian violence and terrorism are countries like "Somalia, Libya, Yemen, Syria, Iraq and Afghanistan," political and economic system have totally collapsed and till year 2016 showing no signs of improvement, other major predominately Sunni-Muslim countries like Pakistan, Turkey and Egypt as well experiencing extreme rise in violence and terrorist activities, growing violence obviously harms economic growth hence reduces or rather decimate economic opportunities, situation in Islamic world between 2012 and 2016 will better be described as extremely chaotic and problematic.

Obviously when there is so much trouble in the country you live in because no one would like to live in such a chaotic situation, in such excruciating circumstances people would want to leave war-zones and move to safe harbour, after all we all care about our personal safety and security.

But here again, very often, when discussion is about Islamic problems, one question comes to mind of many, not just one question but many pressing questions, as we all know that **Islam** a great religion has been branded and promoted as the most peace loving **Religion of Peace**, than, Why so much chaos and distress in so many Islamic countries? Why are Muslim brothers and sisters from war-ravaged and poverty stricken Muslim countries fleeing and wants to desperately move to non-Muslim ruled countries to seek asylum or economic refuge? Another question arises, as to, Why Muslims are leaving Muslim countries and opting to settle in non-Islamic countries such as Australia, Canada, or in America and Europe? Isn't it true that Muslims calls non-believers (all those who do not follow Islam) <u>Kafirs</u> (infidels). These are genuine questions to ask, but, who from Islamic community will answer? Have you ever wonder, Islam the most peace loving religion yet Muslims not safe in Muslim dominated and Muslim ruled countries.

With lot of hopes and dreams, between 2012 and 2015 millions of Muslim migrants and refugees have crossed into Europe, but, what better future and economic opportunities Europe can provide now or in future? As of 2015, as it is things are not rosy in European Union countries, slow economic growth, high rate of unemployment and underemployment, plus environment and climatic problems.

Islam itself a divided house, Islam divided into two faction or sect "**Shiite and Sunni,**" both faction consider each other illegitimate, so Islam is divided along sectarian and cultural lines, brutal Islamic problems, wars and civil wars, sectarian strife in many Islamic countries, Islamic problems have created problems for Europeans and also not spared the Americans, sadly the internal Islamic issues and difficulties have divided and cause sharp division within western countries as well.

While the optimists who allegedly have soft corner for Islam in Europe wants to welcome refugees, and they argue that refugees will in long term help Europe, valuable contribution from large immigrant population will help spur European economic growth.

But another large section of European population do not agree with the optimists, and fiercely oppose any move of providing asylum to migrants and refugees who apparently are coming inside Europe from predominately Muslim countries and majority are followers of Sunni Islam, and they are of the opinion and says "**They are not refugee' This is an invasion, Islam entry is Death of Europe**," migrants pose threat to Europe's millennium old culture and civilization and universal values. Hungarian Prime Minister Viktor Orban has also called the flow of migrants a threat to Christian Europe and has tried to halt it, a position that other European leaders have condemned. Hungary also built razor-wire fence on its border with Serbia and Croatia ending its role of a major transit country for migrants using its land on route to northern-Europe.

Mounting social tension and political fragmentation haunts the European society, Political analysts warns it will make entire Europe less stable and crime rate will increase substantially because of immigration, how it will affect the world's most progressive and democratic European nations by vast inflow of people different in culture, attitudes, skills and economic status. Concern and fears in mind of many Europeans have grown especially since the Paris terror attacks on 13th November-2015, worried that jihadists carrying forged Syrian passports are posing as migrants in order to enter Europe and launch attacks on the Western countries.

Apprehension among Europeans that migrants pouring into Europe from Muslim dominated countries are not ordinary asylum seekers or refugees but **Multinational Islamic Army (Military)**, and will one day conquer Europe and establish **Islamic caliphate**. European observers are of the opinion that the great national cultures of Italians, French, Germans and others may be replaced by new transnational Islamic cultures and identity.

This one question is worth trillions of dollars; "**Will Islam conquer Europe and America?**"

Islam declares war, after the terror attacks on U.S. soil in sept-2001 (9/11), the Islamist jihadi commanders had categorically stated in their propaganda video messages featuring **9/11 terror attacks** in U.S. "we'll not rest till the time we hoist Islamic flags in centre of **Rome** and in **Washington**, surrender before Islam or else there will be consequences," it is therefore no big secret ever since 622AD, Islamists forces wants to conquer the world and establish Islam Sharia rule. The terror attacks on **Twin Towers** and few other places in U.S. was just the beginning, unofficial or some say it was subtly an official start of **3rd WW**, World War III "**Islam versus rest of the world**," the 3rd WW is being fought or will be fought but unlike the previous 2 world wars which were decisively fought in open battle field, the 3rd world war is being or will be fought in rather bizarre unnatural manner, strategists have planned unconventional means and methods to fight the 3rd WW. In 20th century fought 2 world wars the state actors played key role but in 3rd WW it is or it will be the non-state-actors who are or will be playing critically important role. There is perceptible shift in strategy of the Sunni Islamists, since 622AD until 1918 all the wars Islamic army fought were fought in open battle field, Islamist strategists have realized after the fall of Ottoman Empire that Islamic army can't or won't be able to win wars in open battle field in straight fight Islam will be defeated, hence, Islam is waging a low intensity war which is proving to be highly effective and productive, frequent terror attacks in many different parts of the world, lone-wolf terrorist attacks to terrorize and to instill fear in the mind of the entire world's non-Sunni Muslim population.

Millions of people from Muslim ruled countries have migrated to Europe to seek asylum and refuge, and also many more thousands of Muslims have migrated to other countries such as U.S.A. and Canada, not surprising at all majority of the migrants are young boys and men and their age between 14 and 30 years, according to some news reports many of these young men have more than enough money in their pockets loaded with cash to sustain and to meet all types of miscellaneous expenses, sources and also mainstream media have discovered and have reported that most of these thousands of young men and even many women are well groomed and trained militants either member of Sunni terrorists groups such as "ISIS or Al Qaeda or Boko Haram," intense debate is on in social media **"they are not Economic Refugees --- they are Islamic army,"** and have entered Europe to destroy western civilization and conquer Europe, earlier in the beginning of migrant crisis many Defence experts, bureaucrats and politicians in Europe were reluctant and not willing to believe or admit that Sunni-Muslims entering Europe from Islamic countries are jihadists, but after terror attacks in Paris in Nov-2015 and Brussels in 2016, the European politicians and government officials and journalists are/were compel to believe and to report that there is serious security threat from these Refugees pouring into Europe, so, large military unit or to say the Islamic Army is standing in Europe and at least a small unit of Islamic military also present in America enough in numbers to start a full scale urban guerilla wars in European and American cities.

Article title **"The invasion of Europe and America,"** describes the situation; Europe on the verge to descending into utter chaos, These thousands of Muslim "refugees," most of them from the jihad hotspots of Syria, Afghanistan and Iraq, have been pouring into Greece and the Balkans in huge numbers for some time now. But they do not, of course, want to stay in Greece, Macedonia and Serbia. They want to reach the European Union: primarily Germany, France and Britain.

More of these "refugees" arrive every day. Media reports of this Muslim invasion focus on the crying women and children, who seem to have been deliberately brought to the front of the crowd. Clearly the vast majority of these "migrants" are men, and in any case, under normal circumstances, wouldn't you take the women, and especially the children, to the side so that they wouldn't get hurt in clashes with police? Instead, they are used as human shields.

Immigration jihad, or hijrah, is the migration or journey of Muhammad and his followers from Mecca to Yathrib, later renamed by him to Medina, in the year 622 CE. It was after the hijrah that Muhammad for the first time became not just a preacher of religious ideas, but a political and military leader. That was what occasioned his new "revelations" exhorting his followers to commit violence against unbelievers. Significantly, the Islamic calendar counts the hijrah, not Muhammad's birth or the occasion of his first "revelation," as the beginning of Islam, implying that Islam is not fully itself without a political and military component.

And true to that martial aspect of this immigration, the "refugees" have grown increasingly violent. Nonetheless, the enemedia and compromised government officials maintain that if you disagree with letting all these people into your country, you are a heartless hateful racist bigot. But this is as absurd as it is insidious. Imagine if this logic were applied in daily life, if someone wanted to enter your house, take all your belongings and even move in there. Should you be forced to let them in?".......

What worries not only Christianity but other major religious communities such as Judaism, Hindus and Buddhists or even the non-believers atheists is rapid rise in Islamic population, yes, Islam is world's fastest growing religion, Islamist population is increasing at phenomenal pace, and threatening to become world's largest religion outstripping Christianity, unless something dramatically different happens or else by the year 2050 **Islam** will become world's largest religion, for the past Two thousand years or more Christianity has/have vehemently dominated global economics and politics, but today it concerns Christian institutions that sharp rise in Muslim population will ultimately decimate Christianity's control and power in world's economic and politics and Islamists will make Christians second class citizens. Unprecedented power of Islam will potentially increase globally the risk of more religious wars, and precipitate hatred crimes on the streets and at workplace.

Anyone interested in knowing, what is/are the reason for such spectacular rise in Muslim population worldwide? Muslim population growing at 5 to 6% annually, whereas every other religious communities including Christianity, Hindus and Buddhists population growing insignificantly at just 1% or at best 1½% annually, in fact in some countries non-Muslim population is sharply declining, due to economic uncertainty and environmental problems, many young girls and women from non-Muslim religious communities are deferring marriage plan and even if married due to higher cost of living and rising expenses most married females are delaying pregnancy for indefinite period of time, also it has been noticed "most of the non-Muslim married couples are reluctant to have more than one child."

So it is creating serious demographic problems around the world for non-Muslim religious communities or those who are atheists unbelievers, as they all practice strict family planning and birth control, whereas in sharp contrast unconcerned about economic hardship, unperturbed about any kind of social consequences the Islamic folks believe in enjoying sex without any contraception, Muslim religious hierarchy and community leaders as well the politicians openly encourage Muslim folks to have as many offspring as possible, Islamic institutions and Muslim leaders openly in public speaks favouring increasing Islamic population advises Muslim women not to remain single and once married should give birth to at least 3 children, yes its true, Muslim clerics call for each Muslim women to have at least 3 kids if not more, Islam mantra is "more the better," Islam needs higher population of Muslims because only with higher number of followers of Islam, that'll actually help in establishing **Islamic caliphate** (Islamic rule) the world over, Islam's more open agenda is to conquer the world, and for that it needs a big army, people who are ready to sacrifice their lives for the cause of Islam.

*"You are not human if you are not Muslim, if you don't pledge allegiance to 'Allah's apostle **Muhammad**,' than you are infidel and infidels are equal to evil,"* this is how Muslims treat people of non-Muslim communities, though in public Muslims do not admit and agree and if asked they'll vehemently deny, but it is true, that, since childhood every Muslim children are thought to dislike and distrust the infidels (all' non-Muslims), children's are thought and informed "always be on alert and be mentally and physically prepared to serve your religion and make yourself available for Jihad (Islamic holy war or to say religious wars against every non-Islamic communities)."

Sunni-Muslims have problems with everything, they've problems with "Beer, wine, bikini clad girls, women wearing skimpy clothes like short frock, nightclubs and discos, all types of music, artefacts, they dislike Jewish community, they hate atheists and detest gays and lesbians, in super-markets they want Halal food, in cosmetic shops they want Halal (legitimate as per Islamic law permitted by Sharia) cosmetic items Perfumes and lipsticks without any alcohol, pork or blood contains, in airlines while travelling they (Muslims) insist Halal food is served to them, they want prayer hall or some kind of adjustment be made so as to offer their regular prayers at workplace or you'll see them praying right on street pavement or on the corner of the road or in case while travelling they pray on railway platform or at airport lounge," damn it these Muslims are so demanding and fussy want preferential treatments and privileges, irrespective and regardless of which country they are in or live in, no matter where they are, they want everything as per their religion's permissible rule, if their religion 'Islam' restricts them from so many things, than for "what purpose do these Muslims migrate to non-believers progressive European and American countries? Why can't Muslims live as per their traditions in their own respective Islamic countries and do what they like best doing? And allow the rest of the world's non-Muslim population live in peace. Sunni-Muslims desirously find peace in destroying other people's peace.

Greed becomes Good, Good becomes Bad; in 20th century world witnessed two ferociously fought World Wars, in 2nd half of 20th century as well several bloody wars were fought, Korean war, Vietnam war and Iran – Iraq war which lasted for over 8years, each of these savagely fought wars have had devastating consequences, millions of people lost their lives and millions more suffered acute humiliation and extreme economic hardship but contrary to what people at that time had feared none of these wars sparked the much anticipated 3rd WW.

But as it seems like the worse was reserve for 21st century, what started in January-2011 was initially a peoples movement in Tunisia which soon spill over to other neighbouring countries in the region to *Libya and Egypt*, **Arab Spring Revolution** (or call it **Jasmine revolution**), Arab spring revolution was something similar to 18th century French Revolution, local citizens of Tunisia and Egypt demanding greater freedom, democratic rights and accountability, Arab spring was initially a peaceful peoples movement, local citizens protesting against their respective country's dictatorial regimes, but no sooner had the peaceful Arab spring revolution had started the opportunist Islamic jihadists elements seized the opportunity and crushed the peoples movement and turned the revolutionary process into full blown Islamic Sectarian conflict, the Sunni extremist elements using oppressive measures suppressed the voice of innocent civilians who were seeking and demanding more freedom and justice for themselves in several Muslim ruled African and Arabian countries, since 2011 many Muslim dominated countries in Africa and West-Asia have plunged into deeper social and political crisis, the worst hit and most fiercely affected countries are Yemen, Syria, Libya and Iraq, also countries like Egypt, Tunisia, Nigeria, Kenya as well are among countries which have experienced terrorism, brutal terrorists perpetrating heinous crimes and violence.

Between 2011 and 2015 in several Muslim ruled countries in Arabian region and in Africa well over 400,000 people have lost their life, add couple of more Muslim ruled countries like Pakistan and Afghanistan which as well are equally seriously affected by immense terrorist activities and the count of number of deaths increases by another 20,000 at least, thousands more citizens of these violence affected nations are/were wounded with severe wounds and injuries, so much human blood has shamelessly flowed over the years, the sectarian conflict between Shia and Sunni faction of Islam and other extreme and grotesque acts of graphic violence in many Islamic countries situated in west-Asia and Africa, the terrorists activities gained further momentum since the middle of year-2014. Ever so increasing violence and killings due to civil wars and sectarian conflict between various Islamic factions and groups, with no likely possibility or chance of any kind of compromise or understanding between warring factions of Islam and hopes are fading for finding any amicable lasting peaceful solution to ever so escalating violence and atrocities in Islamic countries and worse still terrorists attacks spreading vigorously to so many other non-Muslim countries as well, therefore by the end of calendar year 2015 assessing the ground realties many political and financial analysts intensely started debating whether if the ongoing civil wars and terrorists perpetrated crimes and violence in Muslim dominated countries "was it or if it is?" an unofficial start of 3rd world war. Whether or not, the magnitude of modern terrorism threat and increase in terror attacks and beheadings of kidnapped hostages of several western countries between 2014 and 2015 can be or can't be construed as unofficial start 3rd WW, but one thing is certain that if and when and if at all, it's a big "**IF**," the 3rd world war if at all it happens will certainly will be a battle between Islam versus the rest of the world, it potentially will be "**Islam versus the rest' The Third World War.**"

Between 2011 and 2015 due to increased terrorist atrocities and continuing wars in "Syria, Yemen, Iraq and Libya" millions of citizens in these conflict-ridden and violence affected nations have been internally displaced and have lost everything they had of their own, millions of families having lost their homes and businesses, beleaguered citizens are/were forced to flee out of their respective country to seek refuge in other neighbouring countries.

While millions more have or had taken a decision to abandon their own Islamic countries all together and move to other non-Islamic countries to seek protection and shelter, according to some estimates between 2013 and 2015 at least 4.5 million people from various Muslim dominated African and Arabian countries also from Pakistan and Afghanistan have in search for peace and to find shelter have moved to safer zone and for that purpose they are or were compel to make compelling choices and taking undue risk and spending a fortune, fleeing war and poverty migrants left with no alternative had to take a tough decision to cross across the Mediterranean sea, that's how millions of migrants have entered European shore to seek refuge and asylum in prosperous west-European countries, but the small journey of crossing across the sea for these beleaguered migrants to the European shore has not been without the problems, there were horrific tragic incidents of small size overcrowded boat laden with migrants many of the ill-fated boats capsized, resulting in deaths of tens of thousands of migrants by drowning into the sea.

"This is Real life nightmare I must say," the political crisis as well as religious and ideological differences between various Islamic and ethnic communities in Muslim dominated countries is the worst thing happening to mankind, the so-called Arab spring revolution has indeed turned into Arab or to say Islamic nightmare.

Humanitarian crisis or humanitarian catastrophe it is arguably worse humanitarian problem since the end of 2nd world war, or in some aspect worse than that was experienced during 2nd world war. Wars and religious violence are wild and callous, most of us know that in past and perhaps even in present times in many countries and in many wars and civil wars official Army, insurgent rebels or terrorists uses **Rape as Weapon of War**, but in Syria's civil war apart from Sexual violence a new method of intimidating enemy forces have emerged, **Starvation as Weapon of War**, local citizens in many villages, towns and cities in Syria are or were being Starved, with intention to pressurize rival enemy forces and to punish supporters of political rivals and opponents, not just in Syria but there are unconfirmed reports suggest that even in some villages and cities in Iraq, Libya and Yemen same pressure tactics are or were used of cutting food and water supply with an intention to suppress opponents and to exert pressure on rival forces. Starvation is not a new weapon but a tactic from medieval times finding modern applications. As a tactic, starvation not only weakens your enemy but also places them under increasing pressure to care for civilians within the besieged site.

But as it is said, that, one problem creates many more problems, the refugee crisis in Europe is clearly humanitarian nightmare, but there is another bigger perspective to understand, the Islamic crisis and civil wars in Muslim dominated countries in west-Asia, Afghanistan, and in Africa has enveloped Europeans as well, the inrush of asylum seekers in Europe mainly from Islamic countries between 2013 and 2015, the sectarian conflict and sharp division among Muslims over their religious issues and factional feud of Islam has put European countries government officials and politicians in bizarre situation and compelled them to deal with rather unimaginable predicament.

As it is that Europe has not fully recovered from the 2008/9 global economic recession, there aren't many or rather it will be safe to assume that there are none, no new business investments particularly in manufacturing sector all over Europe, on economic front not much exciting things happening as of 2014/15 there are No new mega business investments planned for starting any big commercial industrial projects in Europe, unemployment rate as of 2014 in few prominent European countries like "Spain, Italy, Portugal and Greece was well over 15%, unemployment rate is even higher among the youths, so unemployment and underemployment is prevalent all across Europe, rising incidents of crimes, crime rate between 2004 & 2014 has risen exponentially in many key European cities. Keeping in mind abrasive ground realities, hence because of increasing flow of asylum seekers to European countries many thoughtful Rightist leaning individual people in Europe are jittery and resolutely against and unwilling to welcome migrants who are/were migrating from Islamic countries.

So to say, that bitter unending Islamic sectarian and internal religious problems have created problems within the European community as well, Islamic problems and massive flow of large number of refugees and asylum seekers from Muslim dominated countries have had brutally divided Europe into two faction, one faction inside Europe are optimists and have positive feelings for the asylum seekers and supports the idea of allowing migrants in Europe and they argue favourably for granting asylum citing reasons that the migrants from west-Asia based Islamic countries will in long term prove to be an asset and will solve chronic European demographic problems, the optimists are of the view that those migrants entering Europe have skills and talent and their talent can best be utilize for commercial purposes by European businesses, but another faction of Europeans largely consist of rightist activist and Far-Right political parties vehemently opposes any move to accommodate such large flow of millions of migrants from Muslim dominated countries, the rightists elements who opposes allowing entry to migrants are of the opinion that Muslims from Islamic countries only have one talent and that talent is **Combative terror activities and aggression**, the pessimists are arguing that in long term the Muslim refugees once they settle in Europe and consolidate their position and forms their community bases inside Europe, the crafty Islamic folks will destroy millennium old European culture and traditions and will decimate centuries old civilization.

Since the German Government between 2013 & 2015 has granted asylum to over 2 million refugees, and provided them shelter and permission to live and work in Germany, large section of mainstream German society is disgusted and annoyed with their government's **Open Door Refugee Policy**, many Germans are apprehensive because of sudden spurt in Muslim population in their country, as many in Germany fear that in long term it would have profound and devastating social and economic consequences, there is apparent fear in the minds of most Germans and also among many so-called patriotic Europeans as they fear that once the Sunni-Muslim folks establishes base of their community in Germany and France, they (Sunni-Muslims) may potentially float Boko-Haram type of jihadist terrorist outfit and those Sunni jihadists elements would wreck havoc not just in Germany but throughout Europe. Now, whether or not if this is unfounded belief and false apprehension among the Europeans or if it is a genuine concern and fear among Europeans that the Sunni Islamic folks for the purpose of Islamization of Europe would start **nasty urban guerrilla warfare** in European towns and cities and turn Germany and France into Somalia and Libya of Europe, but, another arguably the most pressing concern among the European community is that Islamic jihadists may capture young beautiful European girls and women and force them to marry jihadists or make them sex slave.

So there are/were conflicting views and split opinions among the Europeans with regards to granting asylum and to give permission to mostly Sunni-Muslim migrants from Islamic countries to settle in different prosperous European counties and earn their livelihood and their young children gets best education, so that Muslim community folks like other Europeans enjoy every basic fundamental and civil rights as per the European laws.

What has/had further harmed the Muslim community cause are/were the frequent terror attacks by the jihadi Islamist Sunni terrorists, couple of terror attacks in Tunisia killing many European tourists, couple of massive terror attacks in France and few minor but intense terror attacks in several other European countries between 2014/15, and also abrupt behaviour of young Muslim men allegedly found guilty of having Physically Abused and Sexually Assaulted young White European Women in German city of **Cologne** on New year's Eve, Muslims involvement in such barbaric crimes sparked major anti-Islam sentiments all over Europe and also in north-America,

Between 2013 & 2015, Series of terror attacks in many different countries around the world killing thousands of innocent people, --- and beheadings of several European and American nationals allegedly in Syria by inhuman Islamist Sunni jihadists, such inhumane crimes against humanity perpetrated by Muslims has made Muslim position untenable, Muslims have become unpopular and whole Islamic community particularly the Sunni-Muslims have been embarrassed and stigmatized by the acts and actions of their community members, also I would like to point out "all jihadi terrorists groups owes allegiance to Sunni Islam."

Spate of terrorist attacks in several European countries and rising incidents of crimes in European towns and cities has taken its toll on Europe's once thriving Tourism industry, millions of Chinese citizens are worth millions of U.S Dollars and have incredibly high spending and purchasing power, once Europe was most preferred holiday destination for the Chinese, millions of Chinese folks use to travel to Europe and U.S each year to spend their holidays, but sharp decline (devaluation of Yuan) in value of China's currency against major international currencies particularly the "Euro and U.S-Dollar" increases the cost of holidaying in Europe but that's only one small part of the reason, more important reason is safety concern among China's nationals, frequent terror attacks and high degree of crime rate in Europe forced many Rich Chinese to alter their annual holiday travel plans, so since middle of 2015 many Chinese did a rethink and allegedly cancelled any plan if at all they had of spending their holidays in Europe or even in other troubled mainstream tourist destination of the world which apparently are not too far away from shores of Europe countries like Turkey, Egypt and Tunisia, and instead Chinese opts to travel to more safer countries in Asia. While supper rich Chinese prefers to travel to Japan, New Zealand and Australia to spend holidays, the middle-income folks from China prefers to travel to countries like Thailand, Dubai, Indonesia and South-Africa to spend leisure holidays, thereby massively hurting business interest of Europeans as well also of the troubled Islamic countries like "Tunisia, Egypt and Turkey" which as well are considered unsafe due to increase terror attacks and rampant fear of Sunni jihadist terrorists. But not only the Chinese even the rich and wealthy Asian Muslims as well instead of Europe they prefer to spend their leisure holidays in countries like Malaysia, Thailand, Singapore and or in Dubai. So if Europe and Egypt are losing business others like Australia and Malaysia etc are gaining, as there is a saying, "One man's misfortune is an opportunity for another man."

If we are discussing 21st century humanitarian crisis and of Europe's political and economic crisis then it is also important for us to understand little bit of past Europe's history as well, here I would like to share an interesting Article title **"Political Situation in Europe on the Eve of French Revolution,"** "On the eve of the French Revolution the political situation in Europe was remarkably simple. The Continent was dominated by five great powers: Britain, France, Austria, Russia, and Prussia. Their neighbors – Spain, Sweden, and Turkey – had all once enjoyed periods of economic, military, or naval greatness, but by the end of the 18th century had slipped into the ranks of the lesser powers. Most of western Germany remained fragmented into hundreds of minor principalities, ecclesiastical cities, and minor states contained within the Holy Roman Empire. Italy, similarly, contained a number of small kingdoms, some independent and others controlled by

Austria. Europe was overwhelmingly agrarian and feudal, particularly in the east, with monarchs ruling absolutely within their domains. Britain was a somewhat different case: though the vast majority of her people were disenfranchised, the monarchy ruled under constitutional constraints. The nation's prosperity was based not on agriculture but on trade. The process of industrialization, though still in its infancy, was well under way.

A generation before the French Revolution, Prussia, under the ruling house of Hohenzollern, had established herself as Europe's newest great power, having won a series of costly and exhausting wars in which she had taken on and defeated practically every major state on the Continent. Frederick the Great had inherited from his father, Frederick William (1713-40), a highly militarized, extremely efficient state where the landed aristocracy and king enjoyed a close relationship. The aristocracy were freeholders of their land and, in effect, over their peasants as well. In return, the crown taxed the nation heavily in order to maintain a standing army proportionally much larger than that of any other European state. Frederick used that army aggressively: he invaded Austrian Silesia in 1740, and thus began the War of the Austrian Succession (1740-48). This was followed by the Seven Years' War (1756-63) (see Osprey Essential Histories, The Seven Years' War, by Daniel Marston) in which Prussia used her formidable army for the glory of the nation and to consolidate her territorial gains, generally at the expense of Austria. During the Seven Years' War Frederick fought the greatest coalition ever seen in Europe – Austria, France, Russia, Sweden, and most of the German states of the Holy Roman Empire – and survived intact. It was the hard-fought bloody encounters of this war that confirmed for Prussia her place among the Great Powers.

The Russian Empire covered a vast stretch of territory containing at the turn of the century about 48 million subjects, over half of whom were serfs tied to the land. The autocratic Romanov dynasty had ruled since the early 17th century. Russia's military reputation had been won under Peter the Great, who had defeated the Swedes in the Great Northern War (1700-21). Although Russia had briefly fought Prussia in the later years of the Seven Years' War, her territorial gains were made at Polish and Turkish expense during the reign of Catherine the Great (1762-96), particularly during the First Partition of Poland in 1772 and in the annexation of the Crimea, an Ottoman possession, in 1783. Russia fought simultaneous conflicts with Sweden (1788-90) and, in alliance with Austria, Turkey (1787-92). She was ultimately successful in both of these conflicts. When the French Revolutionary Wars began, Catherine the Great remained neutral and she died four years later in 1796 without having challenged the Revolution. That task was left to her son and successor, Paul I, who would finally face France during the War of the Second Coalition (1798-1802). Paul was known for his mental instability and obsession with military matters and was assassinated in 1801.

George III, who had presided over the somewhat different and more constitutional monarchy of Britain since 1760, proved to be one of the French Revolution's most implacable opponents. Political power rested with Parliament and the Prime Minister. William Pitt the Younger had attained office in 1783 with a loyal following in the House of Commons and the support of the crown. Though small by continental standards – with a population of fewer than 10 million – Britain was the world's most prosperous nation. Her wealth was based on thriving trade with Europe and her exclusive access to a vast empire which, in addition to Canada and, above all, India, included newly acquired territories in Australia and many of the bountiful "sugar islands" of the West Indies. As international trade was the basis of the rapidly increasing national wealth, the protection of trade was paramount. Britain's unrivalled merchant fleet, which exceeded 10,000 vessels, could confidently rely on the power of the Royal Navy for its protection. Although agriculture was still important – accounting for one-third of the national product – Britain was the birthplace of the recent phenomenon of industrialization, and its growing manufacturing capacity played a major role in stimulating a booming economy. Britain and France were long-standing enemies, having fought one another regularly over the past century and on opposite sides in nearly every conflict in which the two countries were engaged since the Middle Ages."........

This are defining moments, I call it evolving situation! Conflicting views and varied opinions, selfish motives and purposes, internal rift and confusion among European politicians over drafting more acceptable "European immigration policy," the humanitarian crisis is/was far more severe in 2015/16 than it was in 1945/46 after the end of 2nd WW.

Like many people in Germany and in central Europe in the 1920s and 1930s had a perception, who believed their Race or racial group the "**Aryan Race**" is supreme and better than every other Human Race, arrogant as they were, the so-called people of <u>Aryan race</u> allegedly used to despise every other Racial groups and use to consider every other human Race as inferior and use to say that only their '**Aryan Race**' is the **Master Race**, on similar line like the rightists elements once in Germany and some other parts of Europe firmly believed in their Race "<u>Aryan</u>" as <u>Master Race</u>. The Sunni Muslims outrageously have unofficially declared that there Religious Faith the "**Sunni Islam' is a' <u>Master Religion</u>**" better than every other religious belief and every other religion and non-believers are inferior, so much selfishness that the conceit <u>Sunni Muslim</u> folks without any hesitation calls every Non-Sunni Muslim people **Infidel** and infidels according to Sunni Islam doctrine are considered as evil, thus disrespecting and harming the non-Muslims in any possible manner is not considered **sin** but holy duty of every Sunni-Muslim.

The gulf between Islam and all the other religious communities and ideologies is ever so widening, social, cultural and economic divide, what many intellectuals perceive as incredibly dangerous sign of things that may potentially unravel in coming years and decades, which ultimately would prove to become an end game of human's survival on this wonderful planet **Earth**.

The people from various different religion and non-believers who detest Islam for obvious reasons, normally, they are seen sinking their differences and uniting to oppose the diktat of Islam and of its followers (Muslims) as vigorously as possible, the strong dislike and discontent among masses against the brutality of Islam, to some extent unites them to at least to oppose and talk against the savage crimes committed by Islam and atrocities committed by its followers, but conflict of interest and selfish commercial interest of non-Islamic people and communities have failed so far in evolving any comprehensive and decisive policy to defeat the objectives of the "arrogant followers" of Islamic faith. The *war on terror* started in 2001 against the Sunni Muslim jihadist terrorist groups so far has/have proved futile, it has only resulted in loss of money and lives.

The followers of Islam have time and again have made their intentions clear, that, they are united among themselves and unambiguously moving ahead with a clear motive to destroy whatever is non Islamic and against the very ethics and principle of Islam.

Allah is the name of Islamic God, and the followers of Islam are thought right from their childhood, that, there is no God accept one and only Allah (the name of Muslim God), and that prophet Mohammed (the founder of Islam) is slave of Allah and rest (all Muslims) are slave of prophet Mohammed, every Muslim is made to believe that almighty Allah sent their Prophet Mohammed to the world with a message of peace and as a messenger of god to spread the belief and words of Allah.

Allah is supreme god and prophet Mohammed is his messenger, so all who love and believe in teachings of Mohammed that person/persons is/are the true believers of Allah, rest of the people in this world who do not accept and embrace Islam and pledge allegiance to their prophet Mohammed, those individual peoples and communities are considered by Muslims as non-believers and without any remorse or hesitancy the Muslims particularly the Sunni Muslims call such people Infidels and considers non-believers as Satan (evil).

The chronological account of Islamic terrorism between 2014 and 2016 indicates that Islamist military commanders strategy is to sabotage global economic growth. Frequent terror attacks primarily at soft targets, targeting mainly "Revellers, party goers, beach resorts, hotels, nightclubs and discotheques, airports," all done for the purpose to harm and damage the global economy, to confine people and restrict the movement of people scare them from travelling long distance, terror attacks in Paris in Nov-2015 killing more than 120 innocent people, followed by terror attack in America in **San Bernardino** on 2nd-Dec-2015 killing 14 people, March-2016 suicide bombings in Belgium capital city **Brussels** terrorists blasting city's airport and metro-railway station more than 30 people were killed, just a couple of month later in june-2016 an unprecedented massacre in U.S.A. in Florida town of **Orlando** when a gunman entered a Gay and Lesbian nightclub and killed at least 49 people and seriously injured many more, a month later even more gruesome and brutal terror attack this time in France city "**Nice**," when people were partying and enjoying Bastille Day celebrations an allege Islamist jihadi on 14th-july-2016 deliberately drove a massive 19 tonnes cargo truck into large crowd that had gathered to celebrate and crushed people to death and injuring hundreds more people, nearly 84 people were killed in one of the most horrific terror attack not only in France but in Europe, few days later after terror incident in Nice another horror struck in a small town in France a 84 year old Roman catholic priest was mercilessly killed in Church by allege member and sympathizer of ISIS. Series of terror attacks and a **failed coup** in prominent Islamic country "**Turkey**" which apparently is very close to Europe, since middle of 2015 terrorist activities has increased substantially in Turkey, and one of the most horrific terror attack was at **Istanbul airport** in July-2016 more than 40 people killed, Germany another important and large country in Europe has also suffered extreme pain and experienced violence and terrorist attacks however no major terror attacks but dozens of minor terror attacks and killings.

In 21st century **Europe** has experienced lot of violence and terrorists attacks, but, most vulnerable of all the countries is Europe's most fashionable and glamorous country **France**, *France is particularly targeted severely and ferociously by the Islamic jihadis*, the narcissistic plan on jihadists is to destabilize the most powerful country in Europe which of course is France, Germany may be economic power and large country in Europe but Germany strength is its economy, Germans do not have military power and capabilities, German army is by no means as strong as that of France, France is the only country in European Union which has tremendous superiority in defence technology and has superlative military power, French combative army is strong and experienced, realizing the fact as to how important a country France is and Europe's strength and stability lies overwhelmingly in strong France, therefore Islamist strategists knows it well as in to conquer Europe and America they need to first ensure that France becomes desperately weak and unstable, hence, maximum terror attacks and other unlawful activities of Muslims is enormously concentrated around France and French people are particularly targeted, that's because "Economic uncertainty, political instability, social problems and civilian unrest" in France will ultimately lead to collapse of entire European union, no other country in Europe is strong enough nor do they have expertise, experience and apparatus to fight against Islam's military, France has unprecedented amount of sophisticated weapons and also have large quantity of **nuclear weapons**, so, if "France collapses" entire Europe will crumble and Islamists are well aware of it. **Russia** on side-lines but may take risk and interfere in Europe to fight Islamists forces but as we all know in past Russian army suffered humiliating and crushing defeat fighting war in Afghanistan against the Islamic jihadists in the 1980s which eventually led to disintegration of **Soviet Union** and also Russian army have suffered extreme pain in dealing with Chechens. The Chechen rebels and jihadis made life miserable for the Russians.

Article title "**Muslim invasion of Europe**" writes, "The flow of illegal migrants does not stop. They land on the Greek islands along the Turkish coast. They still try to get into Hungary, despite a razor wire fence and mobilized army. Their destination is Germany or Scandinavia, sometimes France or the UK. Some of them still arrive from Libya. Since the beginning of January, more than 620,000 have arrived by sea alone. There will undoubtedly be many more: a leaked secret document estimates that by the end of December, there might be 1.5 million.

Journalists in Western Europe continue to depict them as "refugees" fleeing war in Syria. The description is false. According to statistics released by the European Union, only twenty-five percent of them come from Syria; the true number is probably lower. The Syrian government sells passports and birth certificates at affordable prices. The vast majority of migrants come from other countries: Iraq, Afghanistan, Pakistan, Eritrea, Somalia, and Nigeria.

Many do not seem to have left in a hurry. Many bring new high-end smartphones and large sums of cash, ten or twenty thousand euros, sometimes more. Many have no passports, no ID, and refuse to give fingerprints.

- The sudden arrival of hundreds of thousands more Muslims most likely prompts Europeans to think that the nightmare will get worse; they see, powerlessly, that their leaders speak and act as if they have no awareness of what is happening.
- Central European leaders and people, who have already lived under authoritarian rule, seem to be thinking that entering the European Union was a huge mistake. They came to what was then called the "free world." They do not seem willing to be subjected again to coercive decisions made by outsiders.
- Illegal Muslim migrants will live on social benefits until the bankruptcy of welfare states.
- In all 28 countries of the European Union, birth rates are low and the population is aging. People under thirty account for only 16% of the population, or 80 million people. In the 22 Arab countries, plus Turkey and

Iran, people under thirty account for 70% of the population, or 350 million people."...............

When Benedict XVI visited Turkey, his main purpose was to meet with Bartholomew I, the ecumenical patriarch of Constantinople and the spiritual leader of 300 million Eastern Orthodox. For a millennium Constantinople was the seat of a thriving empire. It was conquered by Muslims in 1453 and renamed Istanbul. Today Bartholomew reigns over a few buildings and fewer than 3,000 Turkish Christians. The patriarchate exists at the sufferance of the Turkish government and with the reluctant acquiescence of the imams.

Imagine a similar future for the Church of Rome. Imagine, a few generations from now, that Europeans have failed to reproduce themselves and have failed to resuscitate their faith. If present trends continue, in some European countries fully half of the population will be Muslim not long after mid-century. At some point *sharia* will be introduced. Historical legal structures, such as British common law and the Code Napoleon, will give way to the law of the Qu'ran. Year by year the Christian minority will become ever more isolated.

The "rape game" Taharrush is about a large group of Arab men surrounding their victim, usually a Western woman or a woman wearing Western-style clothing, and then the women are subjected to sexual abuse. They surround the victim in circles. The men in the inner circle are the ones who physically abuse the woman, the next circle are the spectators, while the mission of the third circle is to distract and divert attention to what's going on.

If there is enough men, the woman is dragged along by the mob, while the men take turns ripping her clothes off, grope her, and inserting fingers in her various body orifices. Taharrush is noted in Egypt as a kind of "lighter sexual abuse or gang rape" and occurred during the Egyptian Revolution (The Arab Spring) of 2011 in the unrest at the Tahrir Square, where Egyptian women and in some cases foreign journalists were surrounded by groups of men, often having been touched with sexual intent and partly undressed, stripped naked and gang raped. There need not be much overt persecution. An effete population will be disinclined to resist the changes. There will be many opportunistic conversions to Islam. High Muslim birth rates and much-increased Muslim immigration will see to it that Christians become numerically inconsequential. They will be permitted to practice their faith, so long as they do so quietly.

Many point to the rapes in Tahrir Square (in' Cairo) in 2011 and 2013 as cautionary tales, describing the so-called "circle of hell" that women faced then: lone women surrounded by men whose hands groped and pulled, ripped and pressed, and eventually overpowered. A 2013 study conducted after the attacks showed that a stunning 99 percent of Egyptian women had experienced some sort of sexual harassment.

True, these asylum-seekers are not Egyptian, but the signs were there all along. And despite new crackdowns on male asylum-seeker from the region, the problem is likely to continue so long as conservative Muslim men remain among their ranks, finding their way into European cities as new citizens. Observed Brenda Stoter, a reporter and sociologist who has spent several years covering women in the region for Al Jazeera and Dutch newspaper *De Groene,* in a recent essay, "Anyone who thinks that you can bring the Arabic world to Europe without social inequality, cultural differences, and the influence of religion, ignores the facts."

Outlining the fundamental differences between eastern Islam and western Christianity — "culture, architecture, music, gastronomy, dress" — the editorial explains these two worlds have been at war "over the last 14 centuries" and the world is now witnessing a colossal "clash of two civilisations in the countries of old Europe". This clash is brought by Muslims who come to Europe and "carry conflict with the Western world as part of the collective consciousness", as the journalist marks the inevitability of conflict between native Europeans and their new guests. The narrative of an Islamic or Arab takeover of Europe, though hardly new, has gained real traction in recent months, propagated by both xenophobic activist groups as well as populist political leaders and parties. Differences of opinion are being sought to be settled by using physical violence. Arguments are met not with counter arguments but with bullets, To be sure, there are legitimate security concerns posed both by the surge in new arrivals as well as the continuing instability and conflicts in the Middle East.

Sunni-Muslims have problems with everything, they've problems with "Beer, wine, bikini clad girls, women wearing skimpy clothes like short frock, nightclubs and discos, all types of music, artefacts, they dislike Jewish community, they hate atheists and detest gays and lesbians, in super-markets they want Halal food, in cosmetic shops they want Halal (legitimate as per Islamic law permitted by Sharia) cosmetic items Perfumes and lipsticks without any alcohol, pork or blood contains, in airlines while travelling they (Muslims) insist Halal food is served to them, they want prayer hall or some kind of adjustment be made so as to offer their regular prayers at workplace or you'll see them praying right on street pavement or on the corner of the road or in case while travelling they pray on railway platform or at airport lounge," damn it these Muslims are so demanding and fussy want preferential treatments and privileges, irrespective and regardless of which country they are in or live in, no matter where they are, they want everything as per their religion's permissible rule, if their religion 'Islam' restricts them from so many things, than for "what purpose do these Muslims migrate to non-believers progressive European and American countries? Why can't Muslims live as per their traditions in their own respective Islamic countries and do what they like best doing? And allow the rest of the world's non-Muslim population live in peace. Sunni-Muslims desirously find peace in destroying other people's peace.

In several Islamic countries most notoriously in Pakistan "**Blasphemy laws**" are used by Islamic extremists to make up charges against innocent Hindus and Christians in order to steal their property and stir up violence against the Christian population. This includes cases of abduction of women, rape and forced marriages.

Estimated to be five million, the Muslim population in USA as of 2015 is about the size of the Hispanic population 27 years ago, but it is growing six times faster than the national rate, thanks to high rates of birth, immigration and conversions. Many African-Americans view Christianity as the White man's religion and associate conversion to Islam with recovering their ethnic heritage. Thus, to effectively evangelize African-American Muslims. The first actual African-American Muslim sect was the Moorish Science Temple Divine and National Movement of North America, founded in Newark, New Jersey by Timothy Drew (Noble Drew Ali) in 1913. In 1925, the name of the sect was changed to the Moorish Temple of Science. Drew Ali developed the 'Koran of the Moorish Holy Temple of Science' and taught that Allah had ordained him as his prophet to the dark people of America. Ali stated that Negro and Black signified death and Coloured signified something painted. Therefore, the terms Asiatic, Moor or Moorish-American must be used. Ali taught that salvation was found by discovering national origin and refusing to be called Negro, Black, Coloured, Ethiopian, etc. Many converts feel uncomfortable with the term "black Muslim", as they regard themselves as part of a worldwide community of believers who do not recognize "race." However, others are less reticent about associating their blackness with being a Muslim, and believe that **Islam** is the "natural religion of black people" and provides the means for full "spiritual, mental and physical liberation" from an oppressive system designed to subjugate them. The tendency by many in the West to bury their heads in the sand and wish away the reality is driven by fear, unpreparedness for and unwillingness to pay the price that this war will require, as well as general fatigue and distaste for conflict after over a decade of it in Iraq and Afghanistan. The Organization of Islamic Cooperation is the largest and most powerful voting bloc in the United Nations and yet most Americans have never heard of it. Of particular concern is the OIC's ten-year program which amounts to an international effort to suppress freedom of expression under the guise of protecting Islam from so-called "defamation." This initiative, however, is in the service of OIC's long-term mission: the world-wide implementation of **Sharia**, a legal-political-judicial-religious doctrine which favours Muslims over non-Muslims, men over women, and denies basic human rights and freedoms. As practiced today, the **Hijra** strategy is an important part of a covert, *pre*-violent "civilization jihad" pursued by the Muslim Brotherhood. The UN High Commission on Refugees – which, like the rest of the United Nations, is dominated by the dictates of the Islamic supremacist organization known as the Organization of Islamic Cooperation (OIC) – is complicit in the process of bringing Muslim refugees to America. Interestingly, no Muslim refugees are ever resettled in wealthy, low-population density Islamic countries like Saudi Arabia.

"**Jamaat al Fuqra**" is an alleged Pakistani Islamic group responsible for a string of **murders, bombings** and other terrorist acts across the world, including in the USA. Its chapter in America calls itself, **"Muslims of America"** (**MOA**), and actively recruits at **mosques** and prisons, where African-American inmates are especially targeted. Islamization of America is accelerating. In tandem with the spread of **Sharia law in America**'s courts, In the Western countries, few Islamic imams openly preach Jihad - Islam's "holy" war - against us (western civilization). But to Muslim-only audiences, imams do preach waging war against non-Muslims. In some Islam-penetrated Western nations like the UK, imams have begun to throw off the cloak of **Taqiyya** and openly declare war against unbelievers in western nations, even on live television. Islamization of the American media, political and education systems in particular is gaining momentum and confidence, and there is near unanimity that it will continue.

Do **CAIR** (Council on American Islamic Relations) and other activist groups merely want to support Black Lives Matter, or do they hope to recruit blacks to their own cause? In 2014, ISIS used the protests and clashes in Ferguson, Missouri as an opportunity to attempt to **recruit blacks** to radical Islam. But ISIS is a known terrorist organization while CAIR, despite its shady history, is considered by many to be a moderate, mainstream Muslim organization. Thus, if it wanted to convert blacks, it would presumably want to convert them to a moderate version of Islam.

Will Islam catch on with black Americans? A great many blacks in America have a strong commitment to Christianity, which serves to act as a buffer against conversion to Islam. Still, it's likely that Islam will make more inroads into the black community than it has in the past. For one thing, traditional Islam doesn't have the "kook" factor which keeps most blacks at a distance from The Nation of Islam. The NOI belief system includes giant space ships, an evil scientist who created a race of "white devils," and, most recently, an embrace of Dianetics.

Even more troubling, Islamic groups, including **Muslim Brotherhood's** Council on American Islamic Relations (**CAIR**), have penetrated the highest levels of the U.S. government. The White House now has a White House Muslim Advisor, who has counterpart Muslim advisors at the U.S. Department of Justice, the FBI, and the U.S. Department of Homeland Security, where Senior Fellow, **Mohamed Elibiary** declared that USA is an "Islamic country." Much of the money for building mosques, Islamic schools and other Muslim assets in the West comes from the oil rich Muslim nations in the Middle East. And they get their money from the West by selling petroleum oil and gas to European and Americans. Saudi Arabia alone raked in $256 billion from oil exports, and a bulk of that money then was funnelled back out to the West via groups like the **Muslim Brotherhood's**

North American Islamic Trust (**NAIT**) to build and own Islamic assets. Not only have Muslims declared war against us: they already are waging it, burning churches, beheading and/or massacring Christians in Iraq, Syria, Ethiopia, Egypt, Saudi Arabia, Pakistan, Sudan, Somalia, Iran, Nigeria, Yemen, Kenya, Indonesia, Turkey, Afghanistan, Eritrea, Iraq, Bangladesh, Malaysia, Mali, etc.

Black lives matter movement gaining momentum in America, in a similar manner like the "**Arab spring revolutionary movement**" of 2011, "Violent and stealth" Jihadis will use any and every opportunity to gain ground. They are particularly "good" at soliciting and manipulating angry youth – from every class and race – who are misfits or underdogs looking for a sense of purpose and personal power. "Arab Spring" revolutions which were inspired by the Muslim Brotherhood and which brought death and destruction to wide swaths of the Middle East and North Africa.

The move to bring black Americans into the Islamic fold actually predates CAIR and ISIS by quite a few generations. Black Muslim organizations such as Louis Farrakhan's The Nation of Islam have been recruiting blacks to their unorthodox brand of Islam for decades. The vast majority of blacks have resisted the temptation to join, perhaps because of NOI's overt racism, its anti-Semitism, and its criticism of Christianity.

Article title "**Bringing to the life Islamic History of Europe**" has written; "Chronicling the Islamic influence on modern Europe, this evocative film brings to life a time when emirs and caliphs dominated Spain and Sicily and Islamic scholarship swept into the major cities of Europe. The journey thus recreated reveals the debt owed to Islam for its vital contribution to the European Renaissance. The film revisits Spain, Sicily and France in search of the story of Islam in Europe, uncovering an incredible tale of scientific advances and rich cultural influences. To many, East and West appear set on an inevitable collision course, with Christianity, Judaism and Islam locked in permanent confrontation. But on this revealing journey through the common past of Islam and Europe, Rageh Omaar, who came to international attention for his moving accounts of the Iraq war, proves that this is not how it has always been.

Armed with his special insight and knowledge of the Middle East, Rageh sets out from the coast of southern Spain where Muslims first entered the Iberian Peninsula in 711 CE. He travels to Cordoba where he discovers a city once ruled by Muslims that was centuries ahead of any in Europe. Medieval Cordobans trod pavements lit up by street lamps; it would be hundreds of years before Londoners and Parisians no longer wallowed in mud through darkened streets.

From there his journey continues to 13th century Paris, where Christian scholars were persecuted by the Church for trying to apply logic to religious faith. The battle was sparked by the writings of Averroes, a Muslim philosopher from Cordoba whose incisive readings of Aristotle (about what was truth and what was revelation) aroused controversy in Paris and helped launch Western secular enquiry 300 years before the Renaissance, establishing Paris as the intellectual centre of Europe for centuries to come.

Back in Spain, while this intellectual crisis was breaking in Paris, the Nastrid Dynasty of Granada was building what would be the last will and testament to Muslim rule in the West.

Inside the magnificent royal palaces of the Alhambra, Rageh gets to see at first hand the knowledge Muslims possessed in mathematics, architecture and poetry. But in 1492, the year Christopher Columbus set sail for the new world, Muslims lost their last kingdom in medieval Europe to Spain's first monarchs, Ferdinand and Isabella."........

Extremely conservative Islamic religious hierarchy and also many of the so-called moderates Muslims considers western education as well as western lifestyle as imperialist, because they feel it has influence of Zionist Christian and Zionist Jewish culture and religion which could potentially prove harmful to Islam and to its followers, therefore it is no secret that we see it on social media as well on mainstream media the fanatic Islamic clerics trying to persuade and restrain

Muslims particularly the Sunni Muslim folks from going to Christian missionaries manage Schools and universities because it is term as Haraam (illegitimate) according to Islamic jurisprudence and against the Sharia (Islamic religious law).

Now the fundamentalist Muslims may in public protest western type lifestyles and western education, they may curse the progress and development of modern science, Ironically each and every of the Islamic Sunni jihadist terror groups (Islam holy warrior) makes optimal use of modern day and time science and technology, the terrorist can't survive without modern mass communication systems, so they vigorously use more contemporary social media network which helps them immensely in spreading message and propagating barbaric Islamic propaganda, the jihadist Sunni Muslim militants makes extensive use of modern communication devices which are the technological products which apparently are researched & developed largely by scientist and technicians belonging Jewish community, also, when Muslims are sick or injured to cure sickness and to heal injuries they consume medicine which are most likely to be researched and developed by those individual scientist and doctors who by faith or by belief maybe either Jewish or maybe even atheist and non-believers and most likely be made and manufactured in Jewish or Christian owned factories, so these are some of the prime examples which proves how brazen double standards this Islamic people have.

Article title "**The true history of Europe and Islam**" describes; "The true story of Christendom and Islam is the antithesis of such claims. Consider some facts for a moment:

A mere decade after the birth of Islam in the 7th century, the jihad burst out of Arabia. Leaving aside all the thousands of miles of ancient lands and civilizations that were permanently conquered -- including Morocco, Algeria, Tunisia, Libya, Egypt, Syria, Iraq, Iran, and parts of India and China -- much of Europe was also, at one time or another, conquered by the sword of Islam.

Among other nations and territories that were attacked and/or came under Muslim domination are (to give them their modern names in no particular order): Portugal, Spain, France, Italy, Sicily, Switzerland, Austria, Hungary, Greece, Russia, Poland, Bulgaria, Ukraine, Lithuania, Romania, Albania, Serbia, Armenia, Georgia, Crete, Cyprus, Croatia, Bosnia-Herzegovina, Macedonia, Belarus, Malta, Sardinia, Moldova, Slovakia, and Montenegro.

In 846, Rome was sacked and the Vatican defiled by Muslim Arab raiders; some 600 years later, in 1453, Christendom's other great basilica, Holy Wisdom (or Hagia Sophia) was conquered by Muslim Turks, permanently. (Till this day, Turkish Muslims celebrate the sack of Constantinople, which saw much rapine and slaughter.)The few European regions that escaped direct Islamic occupation due to their northwest remoteness include Great Britain, Scandinavia, and Germany.

That, of course, does not mean that they were not attacked by Islam. Indeed, in the furthest northwest of Europe, in Iceland, Christians used to pray that God save them from the "terror of the Turk." This was not mere paranoia; as late as 1627, Muslim corsairs raided the northern Christian island seizing four hundred captives and selling them in the slave markets of Algiers.

Nor did America escape. A few years after the formation of the United States, in 1800, American trading ships in the Mediterranean were plundered and their sailors enslaved by Muslim corsairs.

The ambassador of Tripoli **explained** to Thomas Jefferson that it was a Muslim's "right and duty to make war upon them [non-Muslims] wherever they could be found, and to enslave as many as they could take as prisoners."

In short, for roughly one millennium -- punctuated by a Crusader-rebuttal that the modern West is obsessed with demonizing -- Islam daily posed an existential threat to Christian Europe and by extension Western civilization.

And therein lies the rub: Today, whether as taught in high school or graduate school, whether as portrayed by Hollywood or the news media, the predominant historical narrative is that Muslims are the historic "victims" of "intolerant" Western Christians. (**Watch my response** to a Fox News host wondering why Christians have always persecuted Muslims.)

So here we are, paying the price of being an ahistorical society: A few years after the Islamic strikes of 9/11 -- merely the latest in the centuries-long, continents-wide jihad on the West -- Americans elected (twice) a man with a Muslim name and heritage for president; a man who condemns the Crusades while **openly empowering the same Islamic ideology that European Christians fought for centuries.**

Surely the United States' European forebears -- who at one time or another either fought off or were conquered by Islam -- must be turning in their graves.

But all this is history, you say? Why rehash it? Why not let it be and move on, begin a new chapter of mutual tolerance and respect, even if history must be "touched up" a bit?

This would be a somewhat plausible position -- if not for the fact that, all around the globe, Muslims are *still* exhibiting the same **imperial impulse** and **intolerant supremacism** that their conquering forbears did. The only difference is that the Muslim world is currently incapable of defeating the West through a conventional war.

Yet this may not even be necessary. Thanks to the West's ignorance of history, some Muslims are flooding Europe under the guise of "immigration," refusing to assimilate, and forming enclaves which in modern parlance are called "ghettoes" but in Islamic terminology are the *ribat* -- frontier posts where the jihad is wage'd on the infidel, one way **or the other**.

All this leads to another, perhaps even more important point: If the true history of the West and Islam is being turned upside its head, what other historical "orthodoxies" being peddled around as truth are also false?

Were the Dark Ages truly benighted because of the "suffocating" forces of Christianity? Or were these dark ages -- which "coincidentally" occurred during the same centuries when jihad was constantly harrying Europe -- a product of another suffocating "religion"?

Was the Spanish Inquisition -- also condemned by Obama -- a reflection of Christian barbarism or was it a reflection of Christian desperation vis-à-vis the many Muslims who, while claiming to have converted to Christianity, were practicing taqiyya and living as moles trying to subvert the Christian nation back to Islam?

Don't expect to get true answers to these and other questions from the makers, guardians, and disseminators of the West's fabricated epistemology.

In the future (whatever one there may be) the histories written about our times will likely stress how our era, ironically called the "information age," was not an age when people were so well informed, but rather an age when disinformation was so widespread and unquestioned that generations of people lived in bubbles of alternate realities -- till they were finally popped."............

They (Sunni-Muslims) don't even respect the non-Muslims dead souls, in one of the incident in Libya, it was reported, Armed vandals attacked and smashed the headstones of Allied and Italian service members laid to rest in a World War II cemetery in Benghazi and then posted video of their desecration online. The U.K. Foreign Office said that on February 24 and 26 (2016) hundreds of headstones in two British military cemeteries in Benghazi were vandalized. Markers identifying

Christian or Jewish war dead were damaged or broken. In video re-posted on YouTube the men (including the videographer) are seen kicking over or smashing headstones. One man takes a hammer to a ceremonial Cross of Remembrance. Men are heard saying of the dead, "They are dogs."

When Muslims from Asia or Africa migrates in search for better lifestyle and to find better job and business opportunities to the most progressive nations of the world to countries such as Australia, New Zealand, U.S., Canada, or any west-European countries, with regards to immigrant Muslims, how are Muslims treated? Are Muslim folks well accepted among local citizens of developed countries? Do Muslim immigrants respect the sentiments of local people, are they law abiding? This are some of the most pressing questions that comes to the mind of many of us, are Muslims an asset or a liability for the country they migrate too, or are the Muslims painful Scums, the answer and replies from most people will be that Muslims are liability and scums, they demand too much but contributes too little.

Most obvious fact, that, the Muslims and particularly the Sunni-Muslim folks can't change their religious attributes and cannot ever get rid of their insular beliefs, they find it always difficult to socio-culturally blend themselves among other cultures and civilizations, once the Sunni-Muslims forms a group and community union in whichever country they are in, they will unitedly mess up with others, not all but most Muslims will seldom adopt other non-Islamic cultural characteristics and will always hesitate in appreciating other religions culture and traditions, instead most Muslims with whimsical sense of humour will try to force their barbaric chemistry on others.

The Muslims especially the Sunni-Muslims are always in haste to expand their religion's base and to enhance numerical strength, for fulfilling their purpose, wherever they go they will setup Islamic religious centres and will start preaching their religious theology, they'll lure and systematically pressurise non-Muslim individuals to convert to Islam. Muslims are good at bragging and exaggerating.

Whether the Muslims are in U.S., U.K. or Australia they will protest and demand special privileges for their community, they want Food and beverages, clothes and cosmetic as per their religious doctrine, which means items needs to be Halal (legitimate according to Islamic doctrine), what is not served to Muslims as per their religious rule is called Haraam (illegitimate), Muslims will demand food be cooked and prepared as per "permissible and lawful" means according to Islamic rules or else their sentiments are hurt, they want food serve as per Islamic permissible rules even in the Airlines they are flying in irrespective of the fact whether if the airline is owned by Muslim or non-Muslim countries, which means other fellow passengers are left with no choice but eat food as per the Islamic peoples choices.

Muslims have issues with almost everything, not only they want their own women to follow strict Islamic dress code but they will also have issues with women of other religions dresses as well, Muslims also objects to nightclubs and discos, Muslim folks will object to having any shop selling alcohol or Pork meat in their area.

Muslims are disliked by most because of their behavioural attitude, which is a proven fact, they are rather more ruthless and selfish, while Muslims are extremely possessive and take utmost care in protecting the dignity of their own women, but the Male Muslim folks have indifferent attitude and style of dealing with non-Muslim especially the Non-Sunni females. Most of the stereotypes Sunni-Muslim men have prejudice and believe that flirting and seducing non-Sunni Muslim females is their birth right, even the Sunni-Muslim cleric and priest have allegedly express their view that it is **Ok** for Sunni-Muslim young men to seduce, flirt, marry do anything they like with non-Sunni Muslim females, it will not be considered as sin, because of Sunni Muslim perception that every non-Sunni Muslims are infidels and according to Sunni-Islam doctrine harming the interest of infidels (non-Sunni Muslims & non-believers) in any possible manner is considered as their holy duty (Muslim considers the infidels as evil).

Called as "**Romeos of terror**," various crime investigation team in U.K. have discovered that for decades several group of savage Muslim men mainly from south-Asia have been luring young girls, the girls are mostly teenage White European girls but it has been discovered and found that not just white-English girls but even Hindu and Sikh community girls are lured with money and Drugs and systematically seduced and raped than sexually exploited, some of the U.K. based Sikh girls complain that Pakistani Muslim men woo them seduce them when they become pregnant they compel beleaguered girls to convert to Islam and marry them, in few confessional statement it is also alleged that these monsters mostly Pakistani Muslim men after marriage took their wives to Pakistan than allegedly have sold the Hindu and Sikh girls to prostitution rackets in Pakistan.

The same story of cruelty is displayed in every other parts of Europe by immigrant Muslims, in Sweden the immigrant Muslim population is just 5%, but this 5% Muslim men commits nearly 77% of overall crimes inside Sweden, as per some reports between 2011 and 2014 Muslim men were found to be responsible to have raped more than 1000 Swedish women, a crime investigation report discovered that nearly 300 of those young girls raped are/were 15 years or less in age.

"Love Jihad" as it is called in India, call it Love-Jihad or Romeo-Jihad, apparently in India it is alleged by some right wing Hindu groups expressing their fear that the Sunni-Muslim cleric and priest largely encourages the young Sunni-Muslim boys to lure the Christian and Hindu girls and to indulge romantically and seduce them, once the romance reaches point of no return that's when Muslim boys systematically apply condition and forces the girls to convert to Islam so that they can get married, this is a ploy to increase their religion's numerical strength by converting girls to Islam.

Rape and seduce the girls, tarnish the dignity of the woman to such an extent, create compelling situation for woman to make compelling choice of marrying the ungracious Muslim man, so that the crafty man can further exploit the beleaguered woman.

CHILD brides as young as 12 have been ordered to stay with the men they were forced to marry after European officials agreed to recognize the partnerships. It comes amid fears of a Paedophilia epidemic inside European refugee camps after a pregnant 14-year-old girl went missing from a Dutch centre. The Netherlands is facing an issue of providing asylum to young girls who are married in their homeland but are below the Dutch age of consent. The number of underage girls, some as young as 11, being married to older men has tripled since the start of the war in Islamic countries, Poverty-stricken parents reluctantly agree to it when their savings run out and they can no longer afford to support their daughters. Now a generation of war babies are being born to mums who are still children themselves. A girl aged 11 or 12 marrying a man decades older than her is not a taboo but an accepted practice in Muslim society.

"Soeren Kern **published an article** about child sex slavery in the UK. He focuses on a report about the large-scale "grooming" of non-Muslim girls age between 11&16 by gangs of Muslim men into sex slavery. These men do not prey upon Muslim girls. The government, police force, and media have been "multi-culturally correct" and very reluctant to expose this phenomenon or to charge these men. Many feminists would say that men all over the world buy and sell women, kidnap or trick them into prostitution. And they are right. But they are wrong to refuse to focus on Paedophelia Sex Slavery wherever and whenever this monster rears its ugly head. The prepared report is meticulous. It documents that "officials in England and Wales were aware of rampant child grooming—the process by which sexual predators befriend and build trust with children in order to prepare them for abuse—by Muslim gangs since at least 1988."

Imagine that. Imagine being a young girl abused and the very people you are told will help you close their doors on you and worse still blames you for the abuse! The young women concerned are often seen by the Police as being deviant or promiscuous. The adult men with whom they are seen with are not questioned.

These accounts give us a harrowing perspective of the scale of the problem. How do we safeguard young vulnerable girls from those who want to exploit them? How do we inform the public to recognise a child who is being groomed? What use is all of this if the authorities are not going to help bring perpetrators to justice?

Women captives are sometimes forced to marry their Muslim masters, regardless of the marital status of the women. That is, the masters are allowed to have sex with the enslaved human property. It is one thing for some soldiers in any army to strike out on their own and rape women. All armies have criminal soldiers who commit this wrong act. But it is quite another to codify rape in a sacred text. Islam codifies and legalizes rape. It is disappointing that the Quran does not abolish this sexual crime in the clearest terms: Thou shalt not have sex with slave-girls under any circumstance!

According to news article published in "**Mail-online**" reported; "Migrants are being taught about gay sex, how to make love while pregnant and how to find the female G-spot in illustrated manuals distributed in Germany. Refugees in Germany are being taught about how to find the female G-spot, sex during pregnancy and how to enjoy homosexual sex.

The bizarre project – complete with graphic illustrations – is being financed by the German government.
In 13 languages on the government website **Zanzu**, all aspects of sexuality – from how to enjoy 'the first time' and how to avoid venereal diseases are tackled. Refugees in Germany are being taught about how to find the female G-spot, sex during pregnancy and how to enjoy homosexual sex on a website funded by the government. Topics include sex, virginity, the body and sex, the first time, sexual pleasure, sex during pregnancy and sexual problems and fears. It comes at a time when tensions between migrants and natives are still tense following the mass sexual assaults on women in Cologne on New Year's Eve.

The government said the guide was necessary because many of the 1.1 million refugees who have arrived in Germany since last year (2015) received no sexual education whatsoever in their homelands. And because many hold what are considered 'backward' views towards homosexuals – including attacking them in asylum centres – Berlin decided to issue the charts.
Refugees who have not been in the country long 'will receive discreet and direct access to knowledge in this area', said Elke Ferner, parliamentary state secretary in the ministry for family affairs.

As well as being available online and in some accommodation centres, many doctors and clinics charged with the health of migrants will receive the charts to better inform migrants about sex.
The Alternative for Germany (AfD) party which is riding high, declared the project 'a waste of taxpayer money.'"…

They (Germans) wonder whether the integration policy will be effective in folding potentially millions of refugees, from Syria to Eritrea, into conservative German society. No one wants a repeat of the "guest worker" era of the 1960s and 1970s, when one million or so foreigners, most of them from Turkey, were officially encouraged not to integrate; they formed their own communities on the fringes of German society, where many of them remain today. And liberal Germans wonder whether their country will lose its famously tolerant and open attitude towards outsiders. "Germany was already divided on taking refugees and now they will continue to be divided," "The [Cologne] incident (on "31st dec-2015" when it is alleged migrant Muslim men sexually abused and robbed German girls) is being used by the right wing to start a racist debate." Indeed, those on the far right, like the ultra-xenophobic party known as Pegida – Patriotic Europeans Against the Islamization of the West – hijacked Cologne to pump up the volume of their anti-immigrant war cry.

"German chancellor Miss Angela Merkel" a highly regarded and rated as best politician and most powerful personality not only in Europe but in the world, Ms Merkel remarkably popular public figure and politician between 2010 and 2014, but her popularity took a severe beating and started to dwindle for her alleged softness towards Muslim community and her welcoming migrants and allowing refuge and asylum to those mostly Muslims migrating in to Europe from violence hit and war ravaged, poverty stricken Arabian and African Muslim dominated countries, incumbent German chancellor Merkel's open door refugee policy irked not only Germans but most Europeans as well, once most popular and powerful woman Angela Merkel towards the end of year 2015 became highly unpopular for her allege affection and sympathy for Islam and for helping migrating Muslims. Good times never remains good forever, Angela Merkel was severely criticized not only by German and European people but even politicians of many European countries and also from U.S.A vehemently criticized her for her role in dealing with refugee crisis, many people in Europe says it was Angela Merkel who was sending an open invitation to the refugees, Merkel's open invitation message **"Welcome to Germany" we'll help you all, we have a house and job for you in Germany, it is a good place to be in**," encouraged many beleaguered people from war-ravaged Islamic countries to board and sail toward Europe and headed towards affluent European countries like Germany, Sweden, Austria and Norway etc.

Somewhat similar situation prevailed on other side of Atlantic ocean, like Germany's chancellor Angela Merkel another high profile and world famous woman politician U.S.A.'s **Miss Hillary Clinton** as well is or was accused in America for having a soft corner for Muslims and talking favorably for Islamic causes, both world's leading women politicians Germany's Angela Merkel and U.S.A.'s Hillary Clinton are or were brutally criticized for being more accommodative and helping Islamic causes. The rightist leaning and ultra conservative people in America and Europe are disgusted and dislikes their politicians paying steep refugee bills, taxpayer money being spent on paying hefty bills for cost incurred in providing Food, healthcare, housing, training etc, etc to millions of refugees and illegal immigrants pouring into Europe, that's, what irks the Americans and Europeans

Those migrants who've entered Europe from Muslim dominated Asian and African countries and most of them have succeeded in seeking refuge and asylum in Europe's most prosperous country <u>Germany</u>, for all their antics and misbehavior in open society, in many German cities you'll apparently see banners with slogans and comments written on the walls "**<u>Rapefugees Not Welcome</u>**," in 2016 more Germans who were initially silent have started voicing their concerns and turned against migrants and joined anti-Islam forces, fearing the worse social and economic consequences it would have as a result of expansion of Islam in European society.

Denmark, Sweden, Germany and Norway are some of the European nations which have between 2012 & 2015 seen and experienced unprecedented sexual violence and sharp rise in crime-rate, increase cases of pickpocketing and shoplifting. Some horrific reports alleges that some migrant cruel men most probably from Somalia, Pakistan and Afghanistan have allegedly been found involved in some outrageous crimes, breaking into houses and raping women and sodomize young children and gatecrashing into public toilets and washrooms and forcefully indulged in shameless sexual activities. Not surprising Police authorities in many European countries have advised European girls and women also to gays and bio-sexual to take extra precautions and not to step out and walk alone on roads and streets at nights.

From women's perspective, a woman's most valuable asset is her **<u>Vagina</u>**, but when this precious asset is torn apart by a voracious man, when a man to soothe his mind and for fulfilment of his desire of indulging in sexual fantasy forcefully sucks in his Peni into woman's vagina, what a horrible incident that proves to be for that hapless woman who suffers such excruciating pain, one can only imagine.

A woman who gets raped, have to, for rest her of the life live with taboo and stigma. The effects are deep and long lasting.

This post-traumatic stress can manifest itself in nightmares or flashbacks, where the woman feels she is once again experiencing the attack. "She can smell the alcohol on the breath of the rapist and it doesn't feel as if it is happening years ago.

It has become common place for Muslims to make demands upon others to adhere to their standards. So obscene and common decency are opposing elements, which exist precisely because of their opposition. The shame, feelings of shame, embarrassment, repulsion is typical of the individual when he, against his will, finds himself in front of other people's events do not correspond to their education and culture, and reputed for its scandalous sex education.

Modesty becomes common sense when human society membership shares the same sensitivity towards the female body which in some Eastern societies if not fully covered may be considered obscene. The reference culture manages the lives of their bodies and every aspect and functionality, the speech also closely linked to sexuality.

....

The sad truth is that the dominant Western policy towards the Arab people traditionally has been one of containment. Today many applaud as the people of the region take to the streets to claim their rights, but until recently Western governments frequently acted as if the Arab people were to be feared, hemmed in controlled. The Arab Spring showed that many people in the region do not share the West's comfortable complacency with autocratic rule. No longer willing to be the passive subjects of self-serving rulers, they began to insist on becoming full citizens of their countries, the proper agents of their fate.

Article title; **Avoid a classic blunder: stay out of religion wars in the Middle East**: "Muslims in the Middle East are fighting wars of religion. Like the carnage between Protestants and Catholics that haunted Northern Ireland during the last third of the 20th century, there is little anyone can do until local peoples crave peace so intensely they are willing to cultivate it. History shows that outside meddling only intensifies sectarian fury. Stopping internecine war begins at home. President Barack Obama imperils Americans by trying to excise an abscess that can be cured only from the inside out. The decision to re-engage in Iraq, and the wider Middle East, also contradicts the president's other, bigger objective: to exit the nanny business. The last time religious aggression swept an entire subcontinent was during the Reformation four centuries ago, when Christians hashed out their hatreds much as Muslims of the Middle East are doing today. Islamic State (ISIS), or as the President Obama calls it, the Islamic State in Iraq and the Levant, is fighting to restore a caliphate. Catholics and Protestants spent decades warring over similar issues. Should all Christians accept the same religious doctrine? Should all nations be under the dominion of the pope?

The first Islamic Civil War, from 656 to 661, created two competitive sects – Sunni and Shi'ite. Neither recognized the other's legitimacy.

Sunnis bowed to a caliph who ruled over all believers regardless of nationality. The last caliph was Sultan Abdülmecid II. Kemal Ataturk, the resolute builder of modern Turkey, fired Abdülmecid in 1924. The 400-year-old caliphate in Istanbul vanished. Unsurprisingly, not everyone was happy about the rupture. In 1928, the Muslim Brotherhood began in Egypt. That group and other like-minded sectarian organizations gradually spread into the new secular nations of Syria, Jordan, Iraq and Iran." ------Elizabeth Cobbs Hoffman,"--------

On the larger geopolitical level, meanwhile, one thing appears to be certain: the west will have less impact in shaping the Arab world's future than in decades past. The reasons for this are varied: they include the more complex internal politics of western states, which have been badly affected both by the economic and financial crisis since 2008 and by the costly, inconclusive wars in Afghanistan and Iraq. These factors have resulted in greater caution about foreign-policy entanglements, and this in turn reinforces ongoing changes in the geo-economic balance of power worldwide. In this fluid situation, neither regional powers nor global institutions appear ready on their own to fill gaps in authority or provide new direction.

Decades after emancipation from colonial rule, the quest for independence still figures highly on the Arab agenda, and in this quest the pursuit of authenticity has moved to centre stage. Authenticity represents, of course, a highly complex concept, more complex at any rate than many of its partisans would have their audiences believe. While some debate the relative weight of Arabism versus local attachments (Egyptian identity, Iraqi nationalism), Islamist activists have a simple answer: Authenticity is identical with Islam -- not the Islam actually practiced by the so-called popular masses, an Islam already corrupted by misconceptions, magic and superstition, but the true Islam of the age of the Prophet and his Companions, or rather their image of that true Islam. This Islam, so they claim, is the solution to all problems of private and public life, of state and society, the yardstick by which to measure values, goals and institutions. Western techniques and modes of organization may be acceptable, but there is a strict refusal to adopt un-Islamic values. The distinction at once complicates the matter, for liberal democracy clearly involves both techniques and values.

It is this. If Christian churches throughout U.S.A. trained their flocks in political action, advocated a foreign, fascist political system, preached hatred towards other religions, and sent funds to foreign movements to support anti-American activities, they would most certainly lose their tax exempt status. They would no longer be classified as "houses of worship" but would be classified as houses of political action - actually seditious political action. That is exactly what is being taught and promoted in Islamic mosques and "training centers" throughout U.S., CAIR is being exposed for their seditious actions. In the U.S, Muslims most often work to "influence", or in Christian terms, "evangelize". In political terms, they are lobbyists for their cause. In commercial terms, they are promoters of their cause. Of course, there is the occasional "sudden Jihadi syndrome" that erupts in violent acts such as at Fort Hood. Or intricately planned attacks such as 9-11. In countries with greater concentrations of Muslims, they are more aggressive, practicing more overt forms of coercion often through fairly frequent acts of terror. And in Islamic nations that are threatened with western intervention, terror acts are daily occurrences.

In 2010 Muslims made up 11.7% of the population in Russia, according to rough estimate as of 2014 it has risen to 14%, various statistics proves that when Muslim population hits 5% in any country, that country begins to experience major social problems and violence. "Muslim militants kill the men but take the women to have sex with them. And then after they have used them for a number of months, they're so distraught mentally and physically that then they may let them go or they may kill them (beleaguered women)."

In 15th century came the formation of Muslim Crimean Khanate which occupied the Black Sea shores and the southern steppes of Ukraine. Until the late 18th century, Ottoman forces under "**Gedik Ahmed Pasha**" conquered all of the Crimean peninsula and joined it to the khanate in 1475. During the 16th and 17th centuries, it was an important centre of the slave trade, the Crimean Khanate maintained an enormous slave trade with the Ottoman Empire and the Middle-east between 1500 and 1700A.D in which Muslim merchants exported over 2 million slaves from Russia and Ukraine. Native Russians and Ukrainians, because of their fair skin were in huge demand as slaves (mainly women). Hence targeted for kidnapping and slavery. The Crimean Khanate was a Turkic vassal state of Ottoman Empire during 1478 to 1774, later it was dissolved by Russian empire in 1783. The Crimean Khanate was one of the many remnants of the Golden Horde, the north-western division of the separated Mongol Empire. Located north of the Black Sea, the Crimean Khanate also proved to be the most lasting remnant. The term "Tatar" derives from an old Mongolian tribe. It eventually came to be a term used by Europeans for the inhabitants and warriors of Mongol Empire as a whole, especially the Golden Horde division. The majority of Ukrainian Muslims are from Crimean Tatar background. Because of violent nature of Islam and the kidnappings and forced slavery mostly of women, Islam was repressed in Russia starting from Russian conquest of Kazan in 1552 until the rise of Catherine the great in 1762.

The problem with extremism is that no extremist force or an individual person will ever publicly agree and admit that they are extremists and believe in violence and suppression and that their community members and leaders are oppressors. Every social class and political class blames each other for increase in terrorism and deteriorating natural environment and global warming, "Conservatives blames the Liberals, Rightists elements blames the Leftists, Socialists blames Capitalists, Capitalists blames the Communists, Communists blames Zionists, Christianity blames Jewish and Judaism blames Islam and Islam blames all of the above," despite evident of Sunni Islamic folks responsible for so many barbaric crimes, killings and massacres yet Sunni Muslims pleads their innocence.

Who are terrorists? What is terrorism? This may be simple questions to ask, perhaps some people may conveniently answer such questions, but, **terrorism** is not a simple dictionary word that you simply open a book and find a meaning of it, terrorism has a very deeper meaning and there is lot to understand from many different perspective.

Here couple of pressing questions comes to mind of many; how and for what types of perpetrated crimes should the people belonging to particular ethnic or religious community can be branded and termed as terrorists? How to determine, as to, who are terrorists in real terms? Can we or is it possible to define terrorism? Otherwise the answer is simple > terrorists are those people who kills and traumatizes innocent people and causes destruction to businesses and properties, but opinions are divided large section of society argues that they are not terrorists but freedom fighters and fighting for humble cause and helping their ethnic or religious community, some say it is struggle for social justice, hence one section of society calls people indulging in brutal and senseless violence as terrorists and criminals, while another section of society defends the allege perpetrators and blames rival religious communities or particular country's government for tarnishing their community's image and thereby terms terrorists as revolutionary warriors.

It is because there are diverse interest and so many opposing and conflicting views and opinions, one large section of society calls people belonging to particular religious community indulging in violent and destructive activities as terrorists and criminals, but another minority yet significantly important section of society believes they are not terrorists but warriors and revolutionists freedom fighters and are fighting for the right cause and for social justice for the benefit of their ethnic or religious community or for the basic civil rights of poor and downtrodden.

Radicalizing people of particular ethnic or religious community is not actually work of politicians or religious leaders, it is the naïve and gullible people purposefully allows political extremist leaders or ethnic and religious community chieftains to brainwash them, large section in our society mindless people with utmost interest listens to and solemnly believes every illogical nonsense and rubbish these political extremists and self-seeking religious leaders speaks.

Toxic speeches delivered by hate-mongers only precipitates irrational hostile feelings among people, and that's when people belonging to a particular community starts disliking people of another particular rival ethnic or religious community or communities, this is, what is called **divide and rule**, when politicians and religious community hierarchy and chieftains instead of playing role of uniting people contrary to that plays destructive role of dividing people, spreads fear and creates sense of insecurity among people, and highly brainwashed gullible people makes all the wrong choices and are responsible for giving Political, financial and muscle power to all the wrong people, it is not the politicians or supreme head of any particular religious community who exploits people, it actually is/are large percentage of naïve and reckless common-people who allows opportunists forces and selfish elements to exploit them, therefore this is how corrupt people obtains economic and political power.

"Politicians are not fool, it is those foolish People who again and again keeps voting for the same Political parties and keep electing same politicians."

Not only does the politicians and religious hierarchy that take advantage of unprincipled and mindless people, but Movie stars, sports-personalities as well exploits people's sentiments by playing emotive card, if one large religious community is critical of a particular movie star and accuses and curses him/her of inappropriate behaviour or of corrupt practices, then another community to which the alleged movie star or sportsperson belongs to will sympathize and empathize and whole-heartedly support movie actor or actress who belongs to their own community. This is how crafty individual professional sports personalities and artists plays with the emotional feelings and succeed in mobilizing support for themselves and become successful in life and earn oodles of money and enjoys power of wealth and fame.

Therefore even <u>United Nation Security Council</u> have so far failed to define, as to, who should actually be called terrorists? Unable to decide parameters to judge and declare a particular group or organization of flouting rules and harming humanity for their own selfish interest.

For example, the same alleged jihadist folks in Afghanistan in 1980s who were fighting ferocious war against occupying <u>soviet army</u> were respectfully called Mujahideen (Holy-warrior, guerrilla fighters), but the Russians and their allies and the then Afghan government use to call these mujahideens as Terrorists, while the western countries as well as Sunni ruled Islamic countries use to call the Mujahideens as holy-warriors and saviours of Islam and humanity, but then when in 1990s when the same Mujahideens allegedly formed jihadists organization like "Taliban and Al Qaeda," and when **Osama bin laden** emphatically challenged entire world's non-Sunni Muslim communities and categorically stated that his Al Qaeda group has been formed to destroy everything that is against the ethics and principle of Sunni-Islam, and his Al Qaeda members are **Sacred Holy-Warriors** (Islamic army) and his jihadists are determined to obliterate western civilization, Osama Laden categorically stated his Islamic army won't rest till the time they've achieved their objective to establish **Islamic caliphate** all over the world. So the same people who were once friends and allies of America and other west-European countries now became one of their fiercest enemy, America a super-power country not ready to be pressurized, the than U.S. president "<u>George W Bush</u>" on his part vowing before people his nation and said in 2001 that America would hunt its enemies dismantle and degrade Sunni-Muslim terrorism and the terror network.

So, when it suits your purpose you justify activities of people indulging in abrupt and unlawful activities and call the violent activists as freedom fighters, and if is not to your convenience and if it is to your disadvantage then you brand people resorting to violent means of protest as criminals and terrorists.

To understand root cause of 21st century terrorism especially Sunni Islamic terrorism, we need to touch base with extreme ground realities, it all started when in 1979 the erstwhile **USSR** or to say <u>Soviet Union forces</u> invaded Afghanistan, while a small section of leftist leaning Afghanis welcomed soviet forces invasion but large majority population opposed Soviet invasion, we must also remember that was an era of **Cold-war** between the communist and socialist USSR and capitalist U.S.A and its western allies, hence the Americans as well were severely opposed because they disliked their arch rival Russia (a major constituent of USSR) occupying impoverished but strategically located Afghanistan, so those warlords and political parties fiercely opposed to Soviet invasion inside Afghanistan formed an alliance and were called **Mujahideen**, and these Mujahideens (guerrilla fighters) were openly aided and supported both financially and militarily by Pakistani and U.S. intelligence agency the **CIA**, large amount of funds, arms and ammunition as well as combative and strategic planning and explosive training was provided to the Mujahideens (guerrilla fighters) mainly by U.S. and also by rich Sunni-Arab countries.

Article title **"Why Did the Soviet Union Invade Afghanistan in 1979?"** Explains the reason; "The near seventy-year history of the Soviet Union is one dominated by its tradition of foreign military interventions that spanned most of its existence and stretched geographically from Krakow to the Kuril Islands. Within this trajectory, the Soviet invasion of, and subsequent war with Afghanistan (1979-1989) stands out in particular, as a lasting legacy of the Cold War. Globally, its outcome continues to plague international society in the current struggle between the Western liberal democratic order and Islamic extremism. Domestically, the remains of the war have rendered the nation's political institutions, economy and society fragile, and transformed Afghanistan into a battlefield for factional rivalries and a breeding ground for religious fundamentalism.

The invasion of Afghanistan was the Soviet Union's final foreign military intervention before its eventual dissolution in 1991. Soviet troops invaded Kabul on December 25th 1979, on order from Moscow to replace the radical Hafizullah Amin with the Soviet-endorsed Babrak Karmal as head of the Democratic Republic of Afghanistan. On December 31st, the Politburo announced, that by overthrowing Amin, they would ease the pace of Afghanistan's communist revolution and thereby protect the communist (PDPA) regime from collapsing due to its domestic unpopularity, and thereby ceding to Islamist and Western forces. Although in hindsight this provides the justification surrounding Moscow's decision, it gives little consideration of the concerns that drove the USSR to invade. Expanding upon those factors central to Soviet decision-making in 1979, this essay will argue that the Soviet decision to invade Afghanistan was foremost driven by the security concerns a rapidly weakening Afghanistan, vulnerable to Islamic extremism and Western encroachment, posed to the Soviet Union's southern borders. As the attempts at negotiation and sending advisors had failed to stabilise the PDPA regime from collapse, and consequently facing an increasingly narrowing set of options, military intervention became the favoured alternative. Facilitating this decision was the threat of the 'reversibility of communism' pervading across fragile Third World socialist states like South Yemen, Ethiopia and Angola; the pressures imposed by the Ustinov-Gromyko-Andropov troika in Politburo decision-making, heightened by reports by on-ground Soviet staff and advisors who were increasingly involved in Afghan affairs; and the end of Détente framework following the rejection of the SALT II Agreement by the United States Congress."...........

However, as the Soviet occupation dragged on, the Afghan resistance improved its internal cooperation. By 1985, the majority of mujahideen fought under a broad network or alliance called the Islamic Unity of Afghanistan Mujahideen. This alliance was made up of the troops from seven major warlords' armies, so it was also known as the Seven Party Mujahideen Alliance or the Peshawar Seven.

The most famous (and likely most effective) of the mujahideen commanders was **Ahmed Shah Massoud**, known as the "Lion of the Panjshir." His troops fought under the banner of the Jamiat-i-Islami, one of the Peshawar Seven factions led by Burhanuddin Rabbani, who would later become the 10th President of Afghanistan.
Massoud was a strategic and tactical genius, and his mujahideen were key to the Afghan resistance against the Soviet Union throughout the 1980s.

Foreign governments also supported the mujahideen in the **war against the Soviets**, for a variety of reasons. The United States had been engaged in detente with the Soviets, but this new expansionist move angered President Jimmy Carter, and the US would go on to supply money and arms to the mujahideen through intermediaries in **Pakistan** throughout the conflict. (The US was still smarting from its loss in the **Vietnam War**, so did not send in any combat troops.)

The People's Republic of **China** also supported the mujahideen, as did **Saudi Arabia**.

The Afghani mujahideen deserve the lion's share of credit for their victory over the Red Army, however. Armed with their knowledge of the mountainous terrain, their tenacity, and their sheer unwillingness to allow a foreign army to over-run Afghanistan, small bands of often ill-equipped mujahideen fought one of the world's superpowers to a draw. In 1989, the Soviets were forced to withdraw in disgrace, having lost 15,000 troops plus 500,000 injured.

For the Soviets, it was a very costly mistake. Some historians cite the expense and discontent over the Afghan War as a major factor in the collapse of the Soviet Union several years later.

Bin Laden himself once said ``the collapse of the Soviet Union ... goes to God and the Mujahideen in Afghanistan ... the US had no mentionable role," but ``collapse made the US more haughty and arrogant.'9

Terrorism has in 21st century unofficially become an industry, many adventurous youngsters join terrorists groups or criminal gangs because they feel and see tremendous career opportunities, therefore they do not hesitate taking higher risk all for the sake of earning quick money and for extravagant lifestyle.

Rise in defence expenditure, but drop in earnings due to decline in economic activity therefore lower tax revenue, some of the war-torn and those countries affected by civil war there problems are intense and chronic, those countries whose economy mostly dependent on single source of income which is exporting petroleum oil & gas largely situated in North-Africa and west-Asia their governments have to increase local duties and taxes or have to borrow money from international financial institution or rely on mercy of donor nations, while it's a severe economic pain for common-people living in war-zones, it is moment of glory for many others, because unending wars and conflicts in countries also opens up business opportunities for many large Multinational companies, the demand for arms and ammunition, food and medicines increases, manufacturing and trading companies and power-brokers, military hardware and arms dealers, human traffickers and agents exploits the situation and gains a lot, makes vast amount of money.

India and Saudi Arabia are two of the most prolific arms importers, but other Asian countries such as Pakistan, Iraq and Iran as well are compel to increase defence spending, countries buying more arms, amination and other military hardware, not only countries but terrorists groups as well needs to buy sophisticated arms of course for their terror related activities, all this buying of defence equipment is unbelievably profitable for arms manufacturing and exporting industries, wars and conflicts and increase terrorism saves jobs as well creates more high paying skilled jobs in defence sector, arms and defence equipment manufacturers in U.S.A., France, Britain and Russia makes colossal profit.

Who funds whom? Who pays the bills? How are various terrorist groups and criminal gangs funded? First thing we need to understand is that no terrorist group and mafias or criminal gangs can survive unless they have political protection, support of politicians and influential military commanders is utmost necessary for any group or organization to carry-out terrorist activities in that particular country or region where they want to operate, also it is important for terrorist group to win support of at least one of the ethnic or religious community. So without the support of dominant ethnic or religious community and political patronage no terrorist group can ever survive.

Article title "**State Sponsored Terrorism: Terrorism Research**" explains; "Is there a difference between terrorism and the use of specific tactics that exploit fear and terror by authorities normally considered "legitimate"? Nations and states often resort to violence to influence segments of their population, or rely on coercive aspects of state institutions. Just like the idea of equating any act of military force with terrorism described above, there are those who equate any use of government power or authority versus any part of the population as terrorism. This view also blurs the lines of what is and is not terrorism, as it elevates outcomes over intentions. Suppression of a riot by law enforcement personnel may in fact expose some of the population (the rioters) to violence and fear, but with the intent to protect the larger civil order. On the other hand, abuse of the prerogative of legitimized violence by the authorities is a crime.

But there are times when national governments will become involved in terrorism, or utilize terror to accomplish the objectives of governments or individual rulers. Most often, terrorism is equated with "non-state actors", or groups that are not responsible to a sovereign government. However, internal security forces can use terror to aid in repressing dissent, and intelligence or military organizations perform acts of terror designed to further a state's policy or diplomatic efforts abroad.

A government that is an adversary of the United States may apply terror tactics and terrorism in an effort to add depth to their engagement of U.S. forces. Repression through terror of the indigenous population would take place to prevent internal dissent and insurrection that the U.S. might exploit. Military special operations assets and state intelligence operatives could conduct terrorist / extremist operations against U.S. interests both in theater and as far abroad as their capabilities allow. Finally, attacks against the U.S. homeland could be executed by state sponsored terrorist organizations or by paid domestic proxies. **Three different ways that states can engage in the use of terror are:**

• Governmental or "State" terror • State involvement in terror • State sponsorship of terrorism and extremism.

Governmental or "State" terror: Sometimes referred to as "terror from above", where a government terrorizes its own population to control or repress them. These actions usually constitute the acknowledged policy of the government, and make use of official institutions such as the judiciary, police, military, and other government agencies. Changes to legal codes permit or encourage torture, killing, or property destruction in pursuit of government policy. After assuming power, official Nazi policy was aimed at the deliberate destruction of "state enemies" and the resulting intimidation of the rest of the population. Stalin's "purges" of the 1930s are examples of using the machinery of the state to terrorize a population.

The methods he used included such actions as rigged show trials of opponents, punishing family or friends of suspected enemies of the regime, and extra-legal use of police or military force against the population.

Saddam Hussein used chemical weapons on his own Kurdish population without any particular change or expansion of policies regarding the use of force on his own citizens. They were simply used in an act of governmental terror believed to be expedient in accomplishing his goals.

State involvement in terror: These are activities where government personnel carry out operations using terror tactics. These activities may be directed against other nations' interests, its own population, or private groups or individuals viewed as dangerous to the state. In many cases, these activities are terrorism under official sanction, although such authorization is rarely acknowledged openly. Historical examples include the Soviet and Iranian assassination campaigns against dissidents who had fled abroad, and Libyan and North Korean intelligence operatives downing airliners on international flights.

Another type of these activities is "death squads" or "war veterans": unofficial actions taken by officials or functionaries of a regime (such as members of police or intelligence organizations) against their own population to repress or intimidate. While these officials will not claim such activities, and disguise their participation, it is often made clear that they are acting for the state. Keeping such activities "unofficial" permits the authorities deniability and avoids the necessity of changing legal and judicial processes to justify oppression. This is different than "pro-state" terror, which is conducted by groups or persons with no official standing and without official encouragement. While pro-state terror may result in positive outcomes for the authorities, their employment of criminal methods and lack of official standing can result in disavowal and punishment of the terrorists, depending on the morality of the regime in question."................

Saudi Arabia is a wealthy nation, the largest petroleum oil producing and exporting country in the world, Saudi is also largest arms and defence equipment importing country in the world, Saudi Arabia dominant Sunni nation following

Wahhabi-Islam, Saudi Arabia attacked its impoverish neighbouring country "Yemen," Yemen is arguably the poorest country in the world, Saudi army committed genocide inside Yemen, specifically targeting cities and villages in Yemen which are dominated by its rival Shia community population, between 2015 &16, Saudi Airforce bombarded <u>Houthi Shiite</u> dominated towns in Yemen, not even sparing innocent civilian population, mercilessly killing young children and women, it has been reported at least 8000 people mostly civilians were killed in Saudi Airstrikes, and thousands more suffered brutal wounds and injuries, besides massive loss and damage to properties, Saudi army used same **weapons** that it purchased from western countries like France, Britain and America, while Saudi armed forces inhumanly kept attacking desperately poor "Shiite Houthi" population inside Yemen, the western governments otherwise big advocates of human rights and civil rights maintained stoic silence, did nothing to stop and to prevent Saudi government from attacking and killing the hapless Shiite Muslim Yemeni population.

Injustice invariably leads to rebellion and retaliation, Jewish and Muslim religious wars over the control of <u>Israeli territory</u>, while Muslim say *"the land is not Israel but Palestine, and Israel is rightfully land of Islamists and Jewish have illegally captured their land and made Muslims homeless in their own country,"* but, Jewish community strongly oppose Islamic claim, says, Israel is and always been Jewish territory, cites historic proof from biblical era, Israel was land of Hebrew people, so, allegation and counter allegation, each side not willing to relent hence no peaceful solution found, therefore west-bank and Gaza strip has become a battle ground, **Palestine liberation force** and more militant terror organization **Hamas** fighting against official Israeli army, injustice breeds intolerance and once religious wars starts than it goes on and on for protracted period of time. That's exactly what is happening between two Abrahamic religion **Judaism** and **Islam**, no end in hostility, since 1950s until 2015 thousands of people from both community have lost their life, Islamic terrorists seeking revenge are targeting Jewish population all over the world, attacking and killing Jewish people and desecrating Jewish holy places of worship.

While Jewish and Muslim religious wars continues and no amicable solution being worked out, equally brutal are religious wars within the same religion and sectarian strife between two denomination of Islam the **Shias** and **Sunnis** continues because they as well are unable to find amicable solutions to solve millennium old religious problems and sharp differences over religious issues, the first major confrontation between Shiite and Sunni was on 10th- October-680 AD, on this day Sunni jihadi army slaughtered revered Shia Imam '**Imam Hussein**' in battle of Karbala present day in Iraq, in battle of Karbala Sunni army had mercilessly killed Imam Hussein and more than 70 of his supporters which included his family members, relatives and sympathizers who fought against Sunni army and sacrificed their life, so, ever since 7th century the two main faction of Islam the Shiite and Sunni have never shared cordial relation with each other.

It is goal of Sunnis to wipe out Shia Islam by all means possible, in 21st century, Shia army and militias are fighting fierce battle against formidable Sunni jihadists, the Saudis, Kuwaitis and Qataris generously funding the jihadists to fight multiple battles against Iranian backed Shiite army at multiple locations in west-Asia, Islamic sectarian conflict between Shia and Sunni in "Lebanon, Syria, Iraq and Yemen," continues, between 2011 and 2016 more than million people killed or wounded, millions of people internally displaced, homeless and jobless. Sunni dominated countries such as "Turkey, Saudi Arabia, Kuwait and UAE" are staunch western allies, therefore it is alleged many Sunni jihadists subtly and indirectly receives unflinching support from western countries, strange but not surprising many Sunni jihadi when critically injured or wounded fighting inhuman jihad (Islamic holy-war) inside Syria or even in Iraq receives medical treatments -- guess; 'where?' nowhere else but in Israeli hospitals, yes, it has been reported that Jewish doctors are rendering best quality medical treatment to many of the wounded Jihadis. Secret nexus between Sunni Arab states and Jewish state Israel.

There have been large-scale atrocities on the Continent in recent years—in Madrid, London, and at the Charlie Hebdo offices, in Paris, in January of year 2015—but in the aftermath of this one there is a realization that Europe, its cities, and all those institutions predicated on unending peace are now vulnerable to bewilderingly rapid developments. Turkey is reluctant to readmit large numbers of migrants - but it is under intense EU pressure now to do so. Under the current rules, only migrants who have no right to international protection can be sent back to Turkey. That means economic migrants. The reason is that only one EU country considers Turkey "safe" for returning migrants. EU data shows that 23% of asylum claims from migrants of Turkish origin were deemed well-founded in 2014. Turkey is demanding a high price for its co-operation, arguing that it has already spent €8bn helping refugees from the Syrian war. It is struggling with the influx, already housing 2.5 million in camps. As a candidate to join the EU, Turkey wants to see real progress in its accession negotiations. The EU has pledged that, and is offering visa-free travel for Turkish citizens in the Schengen passport-free zone. Historic tension between Greece and Turkey makes the Aegean operation to stem the migrant flow difficult - as does Turkey's long, zig-zagging coastline. Europe is beset by so many crisis that it can be hard to remember them all. In rough order of prominence, they are: home-grown terrorism, the largest migration of people since World War II, sovereign debt, doubts about the euro's viability, the rise of extreme right-wing parties such as France's National Front, Russia's menace to its western neighbours, growing Euro-Scepticism.

The migrants who embark upon this journey are typically represented as terrorized and impoverished—as people driven (to quote Amnesty International) "to risk their lives in treacherous sea crossings in a desperate attempt to reach safety in Europe." The demographic and economic facts complicate that story. When populations flee war or famine, they generally flee together: the elderly and the infants, women as well as men. The current migrants, however, are overwhelmingly working-age males. All of them have paid a substantial price to make the trip: it can cost upwards of $2,000 to board a smuggler's boat, to say nothing of hundreds or even thousands of dollars to travel from home to the embarkation point in the first place. Very few of the migrants from Libya are actually Libyan nationals.

Article title "The refugee crisis: why we need to speak about corruption," have reported; "Although corruption alone is not a direct reason why refugees flee their countries, research shows it is often a chief contributor to the overall violence and instability forcing people to run for their physical and psychological safety. Widespread corruption undermines the legitimacy and stability of a government especially if it fails to meet the needs of its people. Research also shows that corruption prolongs armed conflict and violence and weakens peace-building efforts. Corruption facilitates cross-border smuggling of weapons and insurgents as well as the flow of monies from contraband activities that fuels wars. The trafficking of human beings as well as refugee smuggling, which has become a multi-billion dollar business, thrives on corruption. Bribery occurs at almost every stage of people smuggling from the start to the final destination.

Smugglers often bribe national and foreign officials to issue fraudulent passports and visas as well as border control and immigration officers to turn a blind eye to refugees as they pass. The lack of safe passage for refugees have forced them to pay as high as **US$3,000** per person to reach Europe. Such corrupt and criminal smuggling rings give refugees the opposite of what they seek, safety. Dodgy **rubber** dinghies, **fake** life vests, or captains who **abandon** their ships, have led to thousands of refugees tragically dying in the Mediterranean Sea en-route to Europe."..........

Along the Balkan migrant route, an undetermined number of men, women and children considered economic migrants have found themselves stranded, their hopes of reaching prosperous northern EU countries dashed by border closures. Greece, with thousands of miles of coastline, is the only country that cannot feasibly block people from entering without breaking international laws about rescuing those in distress at sea. Europe's response to the crisis has been fractured, with individual countries, concerned about the sheer scale of the influx, introducing new border controls aimed at limiting the flow. The problem is compounded by the reluctance of many migrants' countries of origin, such as Pakistan, to accept forcible returns.

Many politicians and also media journalists in U.S.A. and Europe have ever since the start of refugee and migration crisis have been voicing concern and also taunting the wealthy oil rich Arab countries of not doing enough or rather doing nothing to help people fleeing from war torn Islamic countries, accusation especially targeted towards Saudi Arabia the same country which is also birth place of Islam, reminding them of their holy-duty of being more accommodative and so to render asylum and refuge to at least those Sunni folks who are escaping brutality and fleeing from war torn, violence hit and poverty stricken nations like Iraq, Afghanistan, Syria, Libya and also Pakistan, requesting Saudis, Qataris and Kuwaitis to allow entry to migrants in the kingdom (Saudi Arabia) and also in Qatar.

It won't be fair to accuse the Saudis, Qataris or Kuwaiti governments, it is not as if the Saudi government had closed its doors and did not allowed entry to the migrants who are/were running away from violence and wars and also fed-up of poverty and social problems in their own Islamic country. It is so that the last thing a Muslim from Iraq, Syria, Afghanistan, Pakistan or any such country want to do is to seek asylum or refuge in a Islamic country like Saudi Arabia, whether it is deliberate as part of their long term strategy to populate non-Islamic countries or it is unintentional, this is highly debatable subject matter. But Muslims for whatever reasons best known to them they always prefer to migrate and settle in non-Muslim ruled country, therefore their preferred choice is Europe, north-America or Australia anywhere but Islamic countries.

Are Muslims especially the Sunni-Muslims deliberately populating non-Islamic countries to achieve something bigger for their religion in long term? Is the **Islamic army** strategically working on a game plan to take full control of global economics and politics? These questions have meaning but is highly controversial subject matter, controversial topic to debate. But at least one thing the Islamists have categorically made clear they'll destroy everything that is un-Islamic in this world.

But then, as we observe there is so much fighting in Islamic countries itself. Why Islamists can't find solutions for Islamic problems? Islamic wars and problems are as complex as much complex is the conflict in Muslim dominated countries. The reasons for savage differences over religious issues and violence varies from country to country, different Islamic or Muslim dominated countries have different and differing problems. To have better perspective of Islamic problems and reason for wars in Muslim dominated countries; Like for example in countries such as Iraq, Syria and Yemen, it is war for supremacy between two main rival faction of Islam the Shiites and Sunnis, in these countries both the Shia army led by Iranians and Sunni jihadists allegedly aided and supported by Saudis and Qataris are battling out in open battlefields.

While other Islamic countries like <u>Somalia and Libya</u> it is a chaotic situation, complete breakdown of governing system, economic and political system have totally collapsed in these two Muslim country.

In Saudi Arabia majority Sunni population is supressing and humiliating minority Shia community, apart from sectarian rift in Saudi there are many other thorny issues, Cultural, philosophical and religious issues, following and governing kingdom based on Hardline harsh Islamic religious law, discriminating local Saudi citizens because there is no freedom of speech and expression, beheading those who dares to speak against or commit any sort of crime and those unfortunate individuals who are found guilty of having violated Islamic principles, according to reports each year at least 600 people are beheaded in Saudi Arabia.

Egypt known as land of Pharaohs, an Islamic country now, the problem in Egypt is cultural and ideological, country is bitterly divided on cultural lines, a tussle between Moderates, liberals and radicals, liberal thinking Egyptians are in favour of more freedom and secular values, on the other side are forces who wants Egypt to have Islamic religious law and lifestyle as permitted by Islam, so it is more of a cultural problem in Egypt, liberals and secular forces defending themselves from extremist Islamic army.

While Turkey another critically important nation for both Islam and for the western countries, here the problems are different from other Islamic countries. Turkey predominately a Sunni Muslim country, the Sunni Arabs and Turks have serious fundamental "Political, cultural and economic" differences and problems with powerful regional ethnic **Kurdish** community, in Turkey the fight is between Sunni security forces and Kurdish liberation army.

Likewise there are internal rift and brutal differences in many other Islamic nations, no matter whatever differences and troubles are there among Muslims, yet, the Sunni faction of Islam is united in their resolve to establish <u>Sunni- Islam caliphate</u> all over the world.

It is all on record, evidently Islam have increased influence and gain maximum possible control over Africa, many African countries which were once ruled by Christians or Pagans, are now under control of Islam, if we take into account atrocities committed by Islamic forces and militants in Africa, between 1980 and 2015 Islamist militants have terrorize entire north & central African region and also not spared east-Africa, Sunni Islamic army have caused maximum possible damage and destruction to properties and lives of Christians and few surviving Pagan religious communities, rampant killings and massacres and forceful conversions, Christians and Pagans were forced to convert to Islam, those who refused to embrace Islam were mercilessly killed.

"Article **"The Islamic Effect on Africa"** describes; "Only the narrow stretch of the Red Sea separates the Arabian peninsula from North Africa, and Islam reached Africa quickly after the birth of Islam in A.D. 610. Consequently, Egypt was the first country to come under Islamic influence and provided the Arabs with an important gateway into the rest of Africa. The Arab traders were accomplished seafarers who were able to cross this route and the Indian Ocean. They also used the Nile River to take them south. In addition, the prospect of crossing the Sahara Desert to head west did not faze these desert dwellers.

One of the primary effects of the spread of Islam into North Africa was the acceptance of the Arabic language. Language is one of the main cultural influences left behind by most invading forces: the Romans brought Latin to its European conquests, providing the roots of modern Romance languages and much of English, and through political control, the Arabs made Arabic the predominant language in North Africa. There is no other part of Africa where political control went hand in hand with the spread of Islam. Islamic expansion into Morocco also paved the way for the invasion of southern Spain that introduced Islam into Europe."......

As of September-2015, Muslim population world over was 1.65 Billion. Of which Sunni faction of Islam dominating with approximate 1.18 Billion, remaining approximately 350 or 360 Million belonging to Shiite faction of Islam.

Islam is fast expanding its bases and numerical strength in Europe, not only in Europe, worldwide Islam is fastest growing religion, every other non-Islamic religions, have a very tepid growth rate, a rough estimate indicates that all other major religions such as "Christianity, Hinduism or Buddhism" are growing at dismal 0.80% to 1.70% annually, in stark contrast Muslims have higher birth rate therefore world's Muslim population is growing at 4% to 5% annually, so if Muslim folks maintains same population growth rate for few more decades, than a most conservative estimate suggest by year 2050 Muslim population in world is most likely to cross **3 Billion**. So such a spectacular population growth rate of Muslims, do other communities needs to be concern about Muslim population crossing 3 Billion Mark? Again a tough one, a simple question, yet difficult to answer it, time alone will tell.

Islam's problems are complex, when Islam is in trouble, it causes pain and creates problems for the entire world's population. However fast growing Muslim population has helped Islamists gradually gain control of some of the most strategically situated countries in the world. While countries in southern parts of African continent have less Muslim population hence have less Islamic influence, therefore southern African countries are ruled and governed by either Christians or indigenous African religious communities leaders, but story is lot different in rest of Africa, entire Northern, central, western regions of African continent have large Muslim population hence many countries in northern, central and western Africa are ruled by Muslims. Similarly like Africa, most parts of large Asian continent have super-large Muslim population, apart from west-Asia majority of countries in central Asia as well in south-Asia are overwhelmingly dominated by Muslims, in east-Asia as well apart from Indonesia and Malaysia many other countries as well have large Muslim population. So as it is evident that two of the continent <u>Asia</u> and <u>Africa</u> are firmly in grip of Islam, and if current trend persists in Europe, unless something dramatic happens otherwise by year 2070 Islam will be majority religion in Europe, hence many European countries will have Muslim <u>Prime-minister or President</u>, therefore don't be surprise, it is likely that by (year)<u> 2075</u> many European countries will be ruled and governed by Islamic forces.

<u>Numbers game</u>, politics is all about numbers, any particular ethnic or religious community which has numbers or to say have higher population in any particular country, in which case it is all obvious that particular ethnic or religious community will control and dominate that particular country's economic and political system.

In one of the article **"Islam is on the rise in Europe - The Islamic bulletin"** narrated; "Islam is the second largest religion in Europe today. In spite of periodic persecution and discrimination, Islam seems to be not only surviving but steadily growing in numbers of converts and influence. With the Serbian aggression against Bosnia-Herzegovina, a Muslim country, interest by people is growing in learning about Islam and Muslims.

The Muslims in Western Europe are those who emigrated from Africa, the Middle East and the Indo-Pakistan subcontinent after the Second World War.

Due to manpower shortages and industrial growth in Western Europe after the Second World War, substantial numbers of Muslims migrated to Western Europe. These Muslims kept their cultural, religious and ethnic links with their mother countries.

Today these Muslims and their descendants, along with a growing number of native people who are accepting Islam have made the Muslim population the second largest in many parts of Europe.

Austria, Belgium, Britain, Denmark, France, Italy, Holland, Sweden, Spain, Switzerland, and Germany have large Muslim populations which are growing every day. The Muslim community of these countries need separate articles to cover their growing social, cultural, and economic role in Western Europe.

Reliable figures on the Muslim population in Western Europe are not available. However, it is believed that an estimated 10 million Muslims live in Western Europe today. France, Germany, and Britain have the largest Muslim populations. Muslim sources estimate that both France and Germany have about three million Muslims each, while Britain is said to have about two million. As in Britain, Islam has been the second largest religion in France since the 1970's. By the year 2,000, Muslims are expected to make up more than 10 percent of the French population.

By the mid 1980's, there was no Western European government that had not instituted some legal measures to stop further immigration of Muslim people from Asia, Africa and other parts of the world.

Large numbers of Europeans have converted to Islam in the last two decades. Their actual number remains unknown. The majority of these conversions have been made through the efforts of different ways or Islamic Sufi brotherhood and the Darqawiyahs which claim a link with the Arab-Moroccan city of Fez. Most of the Darqawi converts are drawn from the solid professional middle class and seek a return to the early traditions of Islam. European converts to Islam have included a number of prominent figures, especially in the academic life. This group includes

Baron Omar Ehrenfels, the Austrian anthropologist (d. 1930); Vincent Morteil, the specialist on African and Islamic affairs, Michel Chodkiewicz, director of the French publishing house Editions du Seuil; and Roger Garudy, the French philosopher and former communist party member.

Several countries in Western Europe have recognized the Muslim feasts and holidays. Broadcast time has also been allowed to Muslims in France and some other countries. But problems remain. Muslims and Islam are still treated unfairly in the media. Any attempt by a Muslim society to make Islam as its foundation of life is seen as a challenge to western civilization and is immediately labeled as fundamentalist or terrorist."...........

"More recent study and data suggests that **as of 2014** Muslim population in **Europe**, there are approximately 6.5 million Muslims living in Germany, and in France have Muslim population of 6 million, while U.K., and Italy have roughly 3 million each, but maximum Muslim population is in Russia estimated to be about 16.5 million."

During the reigns of the first four caliphs (632-661), Islam spread rapidly. The wars of expansion were also advanced by the devotion of the faithful to the concept of jihad. Muslims are obliged to extend the faith to unbelievers and to defend Islam from attack. The original concept of jihad did not include aggressive warfare against non-Muslims, but "holy war" was sometimes waged by Muslims whose interpretation of the Koran allowed them such latitude. Jihad was directly responsible for some of the early conquests of Islam outside of the Arabian Peninsula.

Expansion of Islam in Europe and north-America, what will be medium and long term social effects? How expansion of Islam in Europe will alter political equations? **They are Migrants or Islamic Army**! The European countries are becoming increasingly unsafe, as it is, Europe has been experiencing exponential increase in crimes and criminal activities, between years 2004 and 2014 crimes in Europe has considerably risen higher, and most of the perpetrated crimes are committed by the immigrants and not surprisingly among the immigrants it is the Muslims who are involve in most of the crime cases, so recorded Crime-Data proves Muslims are perpetrating maximum crimes in Europe.

For Europeans other cause of concern also is very high percentage of youth unemployment, according to some estimates at the end of the calendar year 2014 as much as 30% of young men and women in age group of 18 to 34 were/are either unemployed or underemployed, adding to the woes of the European countries is the inrush of immigrants from Africa and West-Asian Islamic countries, the times ahead, in years and decades to come could be full of anguish and turbulence for the Europeans.

Not much happening, economic growth in Europe is subdued, no major business investments in industrial projects, falling fertility rates, European women preferring to delay marriage and pregnancy, chronic demographic problems in Europe, in contrast the Muslims are profound proliferators, the birth rate and population growth of Muslim community is highest in the world, Muslim community is largely socially conservative, average Muslim girls get married at early age, so you'll find many Muslim women who by the time they celebrate their 25th birthday they are already mother of 3 or 4 children. Fundamental ground realities is what is concerning many in Europe, and European community is divided, while the moderates and liberal thinking Europeans are willing and favouring giving shelter to those hard pressed migrant refugees entering European shore to seek refuge, another section of rightist leaning and conservative Europeans are opposing tooth and nail any move of their respective country government and politicians to provide refuge to migrant refugees, also keeping in mind the fact that many of those who are seeking refuge in several prosperous European countries are conservative Sunni Muslims, the reason why significantly large section of Europeans are jittery and apprehensive is because they seriously fear that once the Islamic folks establishes themselves and strengthen their bases inside continental Europe they will destroy millennium old European civilizations, will profoundly harm European culture and traditions and destroy ancient artistic structures, fears emanates from the fact that Muslims have smashed and destroyed traditional art and culture in many African and Asian countries.

The European society will become brutally polarize on Racial, Religious and linguistic lines, with growing immigrant population and maximum number of those immigrants belonging to the Muslim community. The difference over culture and religion will only grow between the Neo-Nazis and the Muslims in Europe, the European rightist leaning right-wing extremists groups and Muslim community intensely dislike each other, which apparently will potentially increase hatred crimes on streets of various European cities because local citizens will become more intolerant and impatient. Because of lower business investments there are too few jobs available hence lot more people will have to compete for the same available few jobs. With rising unemployment and so much uncertainty in Europe, it is likely that situation will implode and get chaotic totally out of control and Europe would potentially become one of the world's most unstable region and plunge into full blown social and economic crisis, fears of urban guerrilla warfare fought in principle European town and cities looms large, which will be catastrophic and social tension will be many – many times severe and brutal than it was experienced in the 1920s and 1940s. If religious intolerance between Muslims and Non-Muslim communities rises and extremism accelerates, it will potentially create Political instability and law and order problems across Europe, Europe could once again formally become an Axis centre for the official start of "**WW 3**.

How Islam spread in Europe? "**Wikipedia --- Islam in Europe**" writes; "Muslim forays into Europe began shortly after the religion's inception, with a short lived invasion of Byzantine Sicily by a small Arab and Berber force that landed in 652. Islam gained its first genuine foothold in continental Europe from 711 onward, with the Umayyad conquest of Hispania. The invaders named their land Al-Andalus, which expanded to include what is now Portugal and Spain except for the northern highlands of Asturias, Basque country, Navarra and few other places protected by mountain chains from southward invasions.

Al-Andalus has been estimated to have had a Muslim majority by the 10th century after most of the local population converted to Islam.[6]:42 This coincided with the *La Convivencia* period of the Iberian Peninsula as well as the **Golden age of Jewish culture in Spain**. Pelayo of Asturias began the Christian counter-offensive known as the Reconquista after the Battle of Covadonga in 722. Slowly, the Christian forces began a conquest of the fractured taifa kingdoms of al-Andalus. By 1236, practically all that remained of Muslim Spain was the southern province of Granada.".........

Historically the relations have never been cordial between Islam and Europeans, there has always been distrust and hatred and many wars, many times the two opposing armies have confronted each other in battlefield "**Wikipedia "Balkan wars**" has written; "The Ottoman Empire lost all its European territories to the west of the River **Maritsa** as a result of the two Balkan Wars, which thus delineated present-day Turkey's western border. A large influx of Turks started to flee into the <u>Ottoman heartland</u> from the lost lands. By 1914, the remaining core region of the Ottoman Empire had experienced a population increase of around 2.5 million because of the flood of immigration from the Balkans.

Citizens of Turkey regard the Balkan Wars as a major disaster (*Balkan harbi faciası*) in the nation's history. The unexpected fall and sudden relinquishing of Turkish-dominated European territories created a **psycho-traumatic** event amongst the Turks that is said to have triggered the ultimate collapse of the empire itself within five years. **Nazım Pasha**, Chief of Staff of the Ottoman army, was held responsible for the failure and was assassinated on 23 January 1913 during the 1913 Ottoman coup d'état carried out by the "Young Turks."

The **First Balkan War** broke out when the League member states attacked the Ottoman Empire on 8 October 1912 and ended seven months later with the signing of the **Treaty of London** on 30 May 1913. The <u>Second Balkan War</u> broke out on 16 June 1913. Both Serbia and Greece, utilizing the argument that the war had been prolonged, repudiated important particulars of the pre-war treaty and retained occupation of all the conquered districts in their possession which were to be divided according to specific predefined boundaries. Seeing the treaty as trampled, <u>Bulgaria</u> was dissatisfied over the division of the spoils in <u>Macedonia</u> (made in secret by its former allies, Serbia and Greece) and commenced military action against them. The more numerous combined Serbian and Greek armies repelled the Bulgarian offensive and counter-attacked into <u>Bulgaria</u>. <u>Romania</u>, who having taken no part in the conflict, had intact armies to strike with, invaded Bulgaria from the north in violation of a peace treaty between the two states. The Ottoman Empire also attacked <u>Bulgaria</u> and advanced in Thrace regaining <u>Adrianople.</u> In the resulting <u>Treaty of Bucharest</u>, Bulgaria lost most of the territories it had gained in the First Balkan War in addition to being forced to cede the ex-Ottoman south-third of <u>Dobroudja</u> province to <u>Romania</u>."............

What we see is not a lack of solidarity; what we see is a clash of solidarities: national, ethnic and religious solidarity chafing against our obligations as human beings. But it's not just a matter of self-pity. Despite living at the crossroads of Europe and Asia, Russia and the Middle East, many Eastern Europeans are incurious and insular. Building a Statue of Liberty on Lampedusa will hardly be enough to deal with the problem. Libya and Syria are frustrating examples: Neither the European intervention in Libya nor its nonintervention in Syria have been able to stop the wars in Europe's neighborhood. Being poorer than Western Europeans, after the collapse of Communism in east Europe in 1990s and at the time of east-Europe's political and economic unification with west-European nations, now they (east-Europeans) point out, how can anyone expect solidarity from us? We were promised tourists, not refugees. Torn between its moral obligation to help others in extreme need and the practical impossibility of helping everybody.

It apparently is not as if only the Europeans have to worry about with regards to intelligence report that some among the migrant Muslims in disguise are well trained members of Islamic Jihadi army, but they also have to be concern about the home grown Jihadis, the radicalization process in Europe began much before the 2014/15 migrant crisis, Radical Islam has spread and is spreading across Europe among descendants of Muslim immigrants, *Disenfranchised and upset* by the failure of integration in mainstream European society, desperate times call for desperate measures, because immigrant Sunni Muslims felt rejected by the Europeans, many deeply committed European Islamists have adopted aggressive approach, hence many Muslims have taken up jihad (Islam holy war) against western countries and western civilization, these Europe's Angry Muslims or the jihadists are dangerous because they are committed to Islamic doctrine, not only European nations and ethnic Europeans have to fear and worry, but these jihadists Islamic armed forces can enter United States of America without visas. As it is the Islamic jihadi network is or has spread throughout Europe from Poland to Portugal all thanks to Islamic extremism or to say spread of radical Islam among the descendants guest workers once recruited by European industries to shore up Europe's post-war economic miracle. Whether it is in smoky coffeehouses in Rotterdam and Stockholm, or in makeshift Muslim prayer halls in Copenhagen and Brussels, or in Islamic religious bookstalls in Birmingham and London, or and in the prison cells in Madrid, Milan and Paris, immigrants or their descendants belonging to Sunni Muslim community are vehemently volunteering for jihad against western countries, Jihadi terrorists hitting hard at soft targets making Europeans and the Americans equally vulnerable.

A look in the mirror of the past may humble us, whether past history or present times Europeans have seen and experienced it all, in 20th century 2 devastatingly brutal World-Wars were fought which left Europe in smouldering ruins, **Holocaust** arguably the worse human tragedy in human history, disintegration of Yugoslavia and collapse of communist regimes in east-Europe in early 1990s and subsequent heart-wrenching ferocious Bosnian war and Balkan war between 1991 & 2001 in which tens of thousands people were killed and millions were displaced.

In 21st century; Among prominent European cities, London and Spanish city Madrid were the first to have experienced devastating terror attacks by Islamic jihadists, but again in November-2015 terror attacks in Paris in which more than 125 innocent civilians were killed, and few months later March-2016 massive terror attacks in Belgium capital city of Brussels. Brussels is not only capital of Belgium but home to European Union, all major institutions, commercial and administrative offices and European parliament is/are situated in Brussels, so to say that Brussels is nerve centre of Europe. So the Islamic terrorist groups in 21st century are or have been systematically targeting prominent European cities and strategic locations. It is not just killings but Islamic jihadi army motives it seem is to terrorize and traumatize the entire European population.

If we assess ground realities between 2008 and 2015, there's plenty of problems European have to deal with, stagnant and subdued economic growth, appalling job market, younger demographic particularly unable to find suitable jobs and economic opportunities. European economy feeling deflationary pressure, Europe's problem for long has been not inflation but **deflation**, prices of essential consumer products and items are not rising because people as well as businesses are not spending, people are spending less because people do not have more money in their pockets to spend lavishly. And further adding to already heavily encumbered Europeans with all sorts of social and economic problems are large inflow of people migrating from Arabian and African war-ravaged and poverty stricken Islamic countries.

To understand difficult challenges that Europe's economy is experiencing, it is because as we all know that Europeans are well-known all over the world for producing high-quality stuff, high-quality European *consumer and consumer-*

durable products also have steep price tag, world over everyone loves and crave to use and consume products produced and manufactured inside Europe, Europeans are master craftsmen therefore capable of producing superior products, the problem is **affordability**, not many people around the world can afford to buy European manufactured and designed products, Italian designers created Fashionwear and leather products, German industry manufactured automobiles and cars, French made wines and perfumes, Swiss made wrist watch and chocolates and everything that is manufactured in Britain, is what people love to buy for their personal usage and consumption, but the disturbing fact is that 85% of people in Asia, Africa and Latin American countries can't afford to buy superior in quality but mind-bogglingly expensive European industries and designers produced and created consumer products and fashionwear, it is always tempting desire of every Indian or Pakistani nationals or Nigerians and Kenyans to consume French perfumes or to wear Italian designers created Clothes and footwear, but affordability is the deterring factor.

In contrast the Japanese, Korean and Chinese industries produces mass consumption consumer products like for example "Computers, mobile phones, automobile or fashionwear and footwear" which are much more affordable and easy to use, since people can't afford therefore European industries exports less and because Asian industries produce affordable consumer products that's why Europeans imports more wide variety of products from China and other Asian and African countries, and this is what is the reason behind chronic economic sluggishness in Europe and America, manufacturing sector has all but collapsed in U.S. and Europe, therefore less or no challenging job or business opportunities available in America and Europe.

Far too many problems for the Europeans and Americans to tolerate.

First terror attacks in Paris later terror attacks in Brussels, many intellectuals and academicians started debating whether to disband EU (European union), as of 2015 approximately 28 big and small European countries have come together and formed EU (European union), EU is politics and economic union among 28 member states, some argue that longer than expected economic recession and slower economic growth, besides serious economic problems in member country

Greece, and many other problems like rising crime rates, increase in Islamic terrorism, growing religious intolerance, Islamic jihadists openly challenging European authorities that they'll not rest until such time they takeover entire Europe and hoist **Islamic Flag** in Rome and Paris. This precisely is the reason many believe EU needs to be dissolve so that large European nations such as Germany, Italy and France can be free to evolve their own economic and monetary policies, have their own currency and each nation takes full responsibility of managing and securing their respective country's borders, also each country can draft and implement their own immigration policies.

Great Britain (United Kingdom) a very important country and dominant player in international politics, at the time of me writing this book, it is hotly being debated and discussed "whether U.K should remain part of EU (European union) or should Britain exit (Brexit) from EU." Fierce debate among British politicians and business lobby, many favour Britain staying united and strengthen its relation with EU, while those who are not in favour of Britain staying with EU they suggest and advice Breaking all existing ties with EU and have its (Britain) own complete independent Economic, politics & foreign policies, renegotiate trade and business pacts and re-work on foreign policies, those British nationals who were earlier undecided which way to vote and whom to favour, but after terror attacks first Paris and later in Brussels in March-2016, growing feeling of insecurity and anxiety among Britishers hence change in thinking, so more number of people believe their country will be better off alone, immediately after Brussels terror attacks many took it to the social media to voice their concern and some supposedly Britain's nationals were writing comments and posting blogs some of the message were **"We British love Europe and European people but not EU (European Union) we'll be better alone,"** so opinions change rapidly, in our life there is no stability, time changes very fast advantage turns into disadvantage and disadvantage turns into advantage all can potentially happen in matter of moments

Once in a year 1968 British politician **Enoch Powell** in his famous speech commonly called **"Rivers of Blood"** criticizing *Commonwealth immigration and anti-discrimination legislation* he had warned and had said, "allowing excess immigration, United Kingdom was "heaping up its own funeral pyre" bringing major religious and cultural changes in British society." Enoch Powell speech apparently caused political storm and damaged what otherwise at that time was a promising career.

What is "Politically correct is not good for economy," and what is "Politically incorrect is correct for country's economic growth," very baffling isn't it, Britain's government in june-2016 held referendum to seek its country-peoples opinion whether to continue being partner of larger EU (European union), "Remain or leave" the EU (Breixt), on 23rd-june-2016, people of **Great Britain** overwhelmingly and resolutely voted for leaving EU, means people of Britain gave their verdict for **UK** (United kingdom) to break its 4 decade long economic and political association with the EU. Political observers and experts who closely monitors and understands European politics alleges that EU is controlled by people who are inept, inefficient and corrupt, this was one of the principle reason why large majority of people in England and Wales felt and believed that UK as an independent country has a much better future because they can develop their economy and create jobs besides secure the border in much better way. With regards to EU, the trade deals and treaties that **European Union** decision making body signs and trade agreements with other countries around the world, EU's *Economic policies and trade deals* vehemently favours and supports the largest and most influential country in Europe that is **Germany**, German and to some extent French businesses and industries benefits the most from the economic policies of the EU, other member countries of EU such as **Greece** and **Portugal** or even the **Italians** and many other small nations which are part of EU benefits little or gains nothing at all from being member of European Union.

No terrorists and criminal gangs can survive in any country or region for a minute more unless they've political patronage and support of influential people, and **patronage** doesn't come for free, but, with lot of **underhand dealings**, and there is no doubt that after the infamous terror attacks on the U.S. soil sept-2001 (9/11) and thereafter the start of **War on Terror** the *Islamist caliphate movement* has not weaken but only got more stronger, Islamic jihadi forces are moving ahead with strong determination, Islamist movement has resolutely consolidated their bases inside America and Europe.

Islamic religious wars and sectarian conflict creates problems not only for Islam but Islamic problems create brutal protracted problems for the entire world's population, British former Prime-minister **Tony Blair** had once said; "Tony Blair had said that "many millions" of Muslims hold a viewpoint that is "fundamentally incompatible with the modern world." Rejecting arguments that Isis is simply "tens of thousands of brainwashed crazies," he continued: "[Isis] does not seek dialogue but dominance. It cannot therefore be contained. It has to be defeated.".…

Too much high-talks and big claims, but on ground there is no sincere effort being made to curb extremism and terrorism. Ineffective, inept and indecisive politicians and government officials on both side of **Atlantic ocean** in America and in Europe, high-level of corruption and inaction, it is the politicians who are largely to be blamed for Islam gaining strength, Islam is becoming more stronger. Many leading bankers and bosses and managers of biggest Multinational banks and financial institutions have strong links and business relation with politicians and businessmen of Sunni Muslim countries, the powerful Sunni Arab and Sunni Muslim criminal gangs lobby allegedly bribes their way to achieve their objectives, it is alleged the Sunnis are patron and makes generous contribution and donates big amount of money to many political parties and individual politicians and bureaucrats in Europe and America, even the politicians and people of Europe and America admit that there exist a lobby and the "Politicians, bureaucrats and bankers" are more loyal and works to favour the lobby that patronize them than they are for the people and constitution of their respective country.

Politics makes strange bedfellows, politics is an art of making impossible matters possible, politics is not a profession for faint minded or weak hearted individuals, the mathematics of politics always adds up to "2+2=5" and not "4," politics is the game best left to be played by those men and women who are strong minded and have aggressive approach and those who are callous and work with sly motives in dealing with contentious issues concerning broader demographics and every other regional matters. Politicians needs to be crafty in their manoeuvring and narcissistic in pursuing their nefarious motives.

The Sunni Islamic jihadi commanders and Muslim-Brotherhood are tactically clever and champions in manoeuvring their causes, and equally opposite is situation in Europe and America as well also in India the world's 2nd most populace nation, Sunni Islam is subtly growing in strength and the politicians and lawmakers plus judiciary in Europe, India and America are *baffle and confused*, they simply don't have courage and determination to contain the decisive growth of Islam, the non-Sunni Muslim political leaders, lawmakers and judiciary around the world have no *perspective* hence have no *policy to deal with terrorism and Islamic fanatics*, that's why, they've comprehensively failed to evolve any strategy to defeat or at least alleviate the growing strength of Sunni jihadi army.

In 21st century post 2008 chaotic financial crisis and global economic recession and subsequent **Arab spring revolution** that started in 2011 in Islamic world, the economic crisis perhaps may have got over thanks to central banks printing unprecedented amount of cash currency and frequent large economic stimulus package, between 2012 and 2016 almost all the major stock-markets around the world recovered from their 2009 low-levels and are or were trading at all time historic high levels, share value of many listed companies skyrocketed helping rich become super-rich, but there are/were significant negative consequences, apart from savage Religious and sectarian wars and conflicts in Islamic countries, there is and was tremendous social and economic problems experienced almost in every major prominent country around the world.

Commodity bubble burst, monumental decline in prices of commodities of strategic minerals such as "Iron-ore, copper, zinc and bauxite etc plus massive fall in prices of petroleum crude oil and gas, a sharp fall after hitting all time high in calendar year 2012/2013, commodity prices fell to unbelievably low levels, it all happened in july-2014 when the commodity prices collapsed, drop in commodity prices may have resulted in gain for few commodity importing countries but drop in commodity prices caused severe pain to the resource dependant countries, particularly hard-hit apart from several Arab countries that so vehemently depends on oil revenue for their survival other resource rich countries such as "Russia, Brazil, Australia and many resource rich west-African countries suffered extreme depression and economic hardship, **Venezuela** the country that has largest proven oil reserves in the world almost went burst, brutal fall in prices of petroleum oil has or had devastatingly severe consequences on the Venezuelans, Venezuela's economy in 2016 due to fall in crude oil prices as well because of bad management of country's economy is/was all but bankrupt. In 2015/16 the Situation in major resource and commodity producing countries is/was similar to that of the great economic depression of 1930s.

Between 2008 and 2016 apart from economic problems there are/were major social problems, economic inequality gap between rich and poor has got more severe and wider, more people lost jobs and few hundred thousand families earned billions of dollars, rising social problems, profound religious and racial hate crimes and intolerance, increase cases of domestic violence reported, civil disobedience and unrest witness in many parts of the world, "**Black lives matter movement**" activists took it to the streets in the **U.S.A.** after incidents of highhandedness and excesses by Police in U.S.A. images captured in cameras of White-skin-colour police officers found involved in extrajudicial killings of Blacks (African-Americans), in most of the cases it is alleged that the Blacks were falsely victimize and they actually were innocent, for no apparent act of provocation bullets were fired at African-American blacks many innocent blacks allegedly killed in gun violence, *every action there is a reaction*, frequently targeted allegedly by White Police officers, "Black Lives Matter movement" protests gained momentum and its members and sympathizers came out in open on the streets to voice their concern, also there were reported incidents of disgruntle Black African-American turned militant and started firing bullets at White Police officers allegedly killing many White Police officers. Social problems and hate crimes not only in America but elsewhere as well, in India the upper-caste Hindus supresses and humiliates Low-caste Hindus, the members of extremist Hindu organization also targets the minority Muslims and sometimes Christians as well. In Europe the large population of Muslim migrants and immigrants creates many types of social and law and order problems, since 2012 onwards there has been substantial increase in social and civilian unrest in many different parts of the world, as of 2016 global economic and social problems showing no sign whatsoever of abating, situation getting more and more grim and literally getting out of control in many places. Crimes, looting, killings and corruption is rampant, rise in drug addiction among younger demographic and viciously growing unemployment, besides social and economic problems there is even bigger concern about ever so deteriorating natural environment, climatic and weather related problems causes frequent natural disasters and millions of people deprived of food and are homeless.

After the demise of **Ottoman Empire** in 1918 at the end of 1ˢᵗ world-war, the Islamic caliphate movement was halted, Ottoman Empire was the principle power centre of world's Sunni-Islam. Thereafter to pursue forward the Islamic agenda to establish Islamic caliphate all over the world, a small beginning was made in Egypt, when in 1928 "Hassan al Banna" founded **Muslim Brotherhood** as a transnational Pan-Islamic religious, political and social movement, as time progressed and in years and decades Muslim brotherhood has gained enormous strength, Muslim Brotherhood mottos includes "Believers are but Brothers," "Islam is the Solution", and "Allah is our objective; the Qur'an is the Constitution; the Prophet is our leader; jihad is our way; death for the sake of Allah is our wish." Muslim Brotherhood may have been banned or declared outlawed in several countries including the country of its origin Egypt itself, but, Muslim Brotherhood is an formidable organization and its hierarchy and members dedicatedly works for selfish Islamic causes and its network is spread across the world and has tremendous influence world-wide over Sunni Islamists because of its unmatched mobilizing capabilities, most or almost all of the Islamic jihadists and terror groups around the world have close links and working relations with the Muslim Brotherhood.

The terror attacks on U.S.A. soil on September-11-2001 (9/11) was a strong message to the world that Islam is back in business, and challenged the entire non-Sunni Muslim population of the world, jihadi army commanders saying "*this time it will be fight unto finish*," only the believers of Sunni Islam will survive remaining folks meaning all non-believers and opponents of Islam will have to perish, in every Islamist jihadists propaganda video and on social media > Muslim clerics communicates to the world "this world is only meant for the true believers (this mean, those who believe in Islam god '**Allah**' and those who pledge allegiance to prophet Muhammad) and remaining population of the world who do not believe in Islamic god Allah are termed as unbelievers" and all unbelievers are infidels and infidels are according to Islam doctrine equal to evil therefore harming the infidels is not considered a sin by Sunni-Muslim instead it is holy duty of each Sunni-Muslim to punish the infidels in extreme situation even killing is permitted.

Islam considers all non-Islamic religious communities and even atheists as infidels, but within Islam the Sunni sect of Islam considers the entire Shiite sect of Islam as heretics, basically the followers Sunni Islam detest every other religions and non-believers, so here let me also emphatically inform that all the notorious Islamic terrorists and jihadists groups "Al Qaeda, Al Shabaab, Boko-Haram, ISIS and Taliban, etc" are **Sunni Muslims**, yes, terrorism is adopted culture of Sunni Islam.

The post <u>Arab spring revolution</u>, most of the Muslim dominated and Muslim ruled countries in west-Asia and north-Africa plunged into serious political and social crisis, the Islamic <u>religious wars</u> that started in 2011 showing <u>no sign</u> whatsoever of abetting, "Syria, Iraq, Yemen and Libya" are the most brutally affected nations, but several other countries in Islamic world, such as "Egypt, Turkey, Tunisia, Lebanon, Pakistan and Afghanistan" as well have experienced extremely high terrorists activities, two denomination of Islam the Shias and Sunnis are fighting war in open battlefield in Iraq, Syria, Lebanon and Yemen, another dominant ethnic community in west-Asia and Arabian region the **Kurdish** as well are not spared, the Kurdish army and guerillas are fighting multiple wars in Iraq, Syria and Turkey against formidable Sunni jihadists groups and official army especially in Turkey.

Political analysts, intellectuals and defence experts views and opinions are sharply divided with regards to so many conflicts, religious wars and terrorism in MENA (middle-east and north-Africa) region of the world. What are those uncanny reason/reasons for such deadly and bloodiest battles and wars to continue for such longer period? Who is responsible for creating problems in Islam and Islamic world? Who benefits most when the Islamic sects fight among themselves? These are some of devastatingly pressing questions and it concerns us all, than another question comes to mind or rather is compelling us to think, "Is Islam imploding or is Islam expanding? Simple questions yet difficult to find answers, political and defence analyst views and opinions are divided, with grave confusion in their mind as they try to ascertain the real reasons and purposes behind brutal religious wars and sectarian violence in Islamic world.

There are two principle theories and potential reason behind 21st century religious wars in Islamic world.

<u>First theory is</u>: "as always the Muslims famous cliché, it is Zionist Christians and Jewish conspiracy to destabilize Islam, vested interest of world's powerful countries, "U.S.A., Russia, Britain, France and other western countries" have

orchestrated religious wars to divide and to harm Islam, for commercial purpose these western countries wants to save jobs for the arms and defence equipment manufacturing industries, so sectarian conflicts and religious wars besides terrorism in Islamic world provides opportunity to these powerful and influential countries to sell arms and defence equipment to Islamic countries and make profit, the Zionists wants to save Israel and Israelis, and wants to defame and stigmatize Islam." These are some of the key reasons that leftist leaning and pro-Islamists analysts and political thinkers vehemently cites and argues.

The second theory is: "the Islamic religious wars, sectarian conflicts and terrorism is part of Muslim Brotherhood's and jihadi army commanders vicious long term strategic plan to establish Islamic caliphate all over the world, the rule of believers of Sunni Islam, since 2011 all sectarian conflicts and increased terrorists activities and killings are Sham, Phoney wars are deliberately planned by Islamists, it will significantly and decisively help Sunni-Islam cause in long term, and ultimately help them conquer Europe and America, because savage killings and profound violence in Muslim dominated countries, will provide valid reason for Muslims on pretext of personal safety and security citing deteriorating law and order situation, poverty and persecution as genuine and valid reason for large population of Muslims to migrate to Europe and America, particularly large migration of Muslims to Europe will immensely increase Muslim population in Europe, already Islam as of 2015 is 2nd or 3rd largest religion in Europe, further inflows of migrants will remarkably help populate Europe with Muslims.

Increase Muslim population in Europe and America will create many different kind of social and economic problems, just to put things in perspective, the bigger the social and economic problems, and increase in islamophobia, the more it helps Sunni Islam causes, Muslims are so to say 'smooth-operators,' they are clever and notorious trouble creators, once Islamists settles and establish their bases and consolidate their position in Europe and America, than in anguish and disgust many Europeans especially the white-skin colour Europeans will be compel to leave Europe and start migrating to other countries in search for better living conditions and exciting economic opportunities, the potential exodus of Europeans from Europe besides slow growth in birth-rate, European women differing pregnancy, and aging European population, and in contrast the increase birth-rate of Muslims, Muslim women getting married at much younger age and becoming mother of 3 or 4 children by the time her age is 28 years, so all these combination of factors will by the end of 21st century and start of 22nd century will make Islam largest religion in Europe and perhaps similar strategy will help Islam considerably increase Muslim population in America, this will help Sunni-Islam conveniently and comprehensively conquer Europe and America."

When Muslim Brotherhood was founded in 1920s, it is alleged that it had planned and prepared a 150 to 200 years long term strategic plan, it has always been goal of Islamists to increase their religion's population, therefore Muslim Brotherhood's allege strategy is to infiltrate as many Muslims inside Europe and America, infiltrate so that Muslims becomes integral part of Europe's and Americas social and economic system, Muslims infiltrates education system and governmental departments, Muslims also participates in political movements and become law makers in different European countries and in U.S., and Canada, Muslims starts working as social workers and starts their own NGO,s to help common people so that to gain sympathy and good-will among local citizens, Muslims gets jobs in banks and financial institutions and of course in mainstream media, so with Muslims well positioned inside Europe and America, they can prepare for final assault to conquer Europe and America,

Western countries in a way inadvertently but determinedly are helping Muslim Brotherhood's nefarious causes, each year, annually western countries such as U.S.A., Britain, European-union, also Japan and China besides international financial institutions like World-Bank and IMF (international monetary fund), all these financial institutions and rich countries provides Tens of billions of U.S. Dollars in humanitarian and other form of economic help and soft loans to so many Islamic countries, "Turkey, Pakistan, Egypt, Afghanistan and Jordan" are some of the prominent countries that receives Billions of Dollars of economic aid and unprecedented amount of money for other types of humanitarian and development purpose, from such large amount of money that these Islamic countries receives, so, instead of using money productively for helping its citizens and developing their country by improving public infrastructure and starting new industries and businesses to create jobs and business opportunities, significantly large percentage of money is allegedly diverted towards **Islam's jihadi project**, yes, the Billions of Dollars these Muslim countries receives, significantly large amount of money is allegedly diverted and used for financing terrorism and extremism, to wage **religious wars** against non-Muslim communities.

Many Sunni Muslim countries like "Turkey, Pakistan, Saudi Arabia, Egypt, etc" have strategic Defence pact and agreement signed with leading western countries, as part of defence deal powerful industrialized nations such as "U.S.A., Britain and France" provides extensive military aid and supply of sophisticated arms and defence equipment to so many Islamic countries, besides sharing of military secrets and information, more importantly high ranking military officials and security experts renders superlative combative training to official army of several Islamic countries with whom they have defence ties, so, several prominent Sunni Muslim countries are large recipients of America's military aid. Now, this is where trouble begins, the high quality combative training and arms that Sunni Muslim countries receives are than allegedly passed on to the Jihadists or to say Islamic terrorists groups, so, basically it is alleged that all the financial support and economic aid and military training and arms these Islamic countries receives from western countries, allegedly is used against western countries by Sunni Islamic terrorists to destroy western culture and civilization.

The Europeans and Americans so to say *have dig their own grave*, Muslim-brotherhood and other Islamist institutions have successfully outwitted and outsmarted the naïve and gullible American and European politicians, therefore not surprising that even the European and American population have started accusing and cursing their politicians openly blaming them for surrendering before Islam, and politicians as well have started to admit that Europe and America's political and economic system is biased "therefore its feeble and devastatingly vulnerable," Islam is growing in strength, as a consequence of **war on terror** started in 2001 against the so-called radical Islam, on the contrary **"Islam has become more stronger"** than ever before, Europe and America marred by corruption have become increasingly weaker.

As part of their strategy Muslim Brotherhood and Islamic institutions wants it to become **"Islam versus the rest,"** **islamophobia** actually helps Islamic causes, the more a large section of society curses and discriminates Muslims, another section of society vehemently comes forwards to empathize and sympathize with Islam and shows solidarity and pledge their support to Muslims, that's what, makes Sunni-Muslim youngsters more determined to fight holy religious wars.

The terror attacks on American soil in Sept-2001 (9/11) were no ordinary terror attacks but it was a subtle start of the 'third world war,' Islam versus the rest, the Jihadists have spared no one, every prominent country around the world have been targeted, "London, Mumbai, Madrid, Paris, Nairobi, Brussels, Orlando and San Bernardino" are some of the key cities among so many more cities in so many different parts of the world that have been between 2002 and 2016 experienced savage terror attacks, Sunni terrorists committing barbaric crimes of killing thousands of innocent people, and Islamic jihadi army commanders making it clear that their ambitions and ultimate goal is to **hoist Islamic flag** in centre of **Paris** and in U.S. capital city **Washington.**

Muslim Brotherhood project '*Civilization-Jihadist Process,*' means the jihadi army must understand that their work in America and in Europe is kind of grand jihad in eliminating and destroying western civilization from within and sabotaging its miserable house by their hands and the hands of believers of Islam, **"Allah's religion Islam will be victorious and all other religions will be defeated."**

Chaos and unrest among non-Muslim communities that to in non-Islamic countries also purposefully helps Islamic caliphate movement, Islam's only agenda is to destroy everything in this world that is un-Islamic and establish totalitarian **Islamic Caliphate** (Islamic rule based on Sharia) all over the world, the more there is economic uncertainty, political instability and civil unrest that much more it helps the jihadists and terrorists, when in July-2014 petroleum crude oil and gas prices fell and fell sharply and sustained the lower levels for longer than expected time, many political observers and intellectuals felt and believed that massive fall in oil prices will deprive the jihadists and Sunni terrorist groups of resources and thereby substantially reduce Sunni extremism because many believed that large oil producing Sunni countries such as "Saudi Arabia, Qatar and Kuwait" will earn less oil revenue hence will have little or no money to fund and finance the jihadists organizations and other Islamic institutions, as to what analysts initially had thought contrary to that exactly the opposite happened, Sunni-Muslim terrorism and jihadists became more restless therefore Sunni terrorism since 2014 is more ferocious and violent like never before, Sunni-Islam extremism moving ahead belligerently with full force more incidents of Fedayeen attacks and lone-wolf pressed into Islamic holy-religious service for killings and beheadings of non-believers of Islam, and more frequent are terror attacks throughout the world, Sunni jihadi army fighting bloodiest **religious wars** with rival Shia military in

"Iraq, Syria, Lebanon and Yemen," there is/was extreme increase in violence and terror attacks in other prominent Islamic countries like "Turkey, Libya, Afghanistan and Somalia," and so many other Muslim dominated countries.

Another largely Muslim dominated country Bangladesh, otherwise the Bangladeshi are Bangla speaking peace loving and secular people who love Art, literature and culture, but since 2013 Islamists jihadi movement has gained momentum and many Bangladeshi nationals shifted their loyalty towards Sunni-Islamic movement, strange but not surprising many well-educated and qualified, tech-savvy youngsters hailing from well-to-do upper-middle class families took up arms in their hands for cause of their religion "**Islam**," Sunni jihadists elements in Bangladesh pledging their allegiance to either ISIS or Al Qaeda targets people and religious priests belonging to mainly minority Hindus, Christians and Buddhists communities, also the jihadists do not spare and kills the atheists and secular people, suppresses freedom of speech and expression by targeting liberal thinking people who by profession are "writers, journalists or artists," worst still knowing the fact how important foreign direct investment is for country's economic growth and job creation in their country, yet, jihadists terrorists kills foreign nationals scaring away foreigners from travelling to their country, thereby harming economic growth prospects.

Pakistan and Bangladesh these two densely populated Muslim dominated countries have emerged as major low-cost manufacturing hub, manufacturing industries have excellent future, "Garments, textiles, leather products, footwear and sportswear" are manufactured in countries like Pakistan and Bangladesh in large quantity and exported world over, but, frequent terror attacks, increase terrorist activities and implementation of barbaric Islamic religious laws, atrocities against women and exploitation of children, humiliation of minority communities, will eventually dither foreign Multinational companies from doing business in such troublesome Islamic countries, so, the jihadists and Islamic clerics are responsible for destroying livelihood of Muslims.

The Islamists jihadists and Muslim-brotherhood strategy is simple, hit hard and harm the economy, chaos and uncertainty, social problems and higher unemployment in Muslim dominated countries, will be a catalysts for Muslims from Asia and Africa to migrate to America and Europe, the jihadists wants large Muslim population to infiltrate in non-Islamic countries, a well calibrated and thoughtful strategy of the Islamists caliphate movement bid to conquer the world is to harm world's economic growth, when there is absolute chaos and panic in the world, when people across the world are frighten and fearful, that is what helps Islam to take advantage of the grim situation and it helps them to destroy other civilizations and religions.

"United States of America" Americans boast with pride says that U.S. is the only super power nation left in the world, Is U.S.A. by any mean a super power nation? Who thinks so? In social media as well in news reports in mainstream media we listen and see images of what real America is all about, "Make America Great again --- Make America Work again --- Make America First again ---- Make America Safe again," these political messages and slogans, these desperate messages and slogans is what Americans are chanting, it only reflects there is so much pessimism among the Americans themselves or at least large section of American society thinks so that things are less satisfactory and all is not well inside the great country of opportunity the "U.S.A.," politicians and scholars especially the rightists leaning politicians and intellectuals thinks that all the Trade treaties and Defence pacts that U.S.A. has signed with other countries needs to be scraped as they are unfavourable and U.S. is seriously in disadvantageous position, U.S.A. is simply paying fat bills for the safety and security of other nations and U.S businesses and industries are gaining less and other countries businesses are getting more benefits, many politicians and scholars suggest defence pact with U.S.A.'s allies as well as trade treaties needs to be renegotiated and U.S. government must ensure Americans get a fair deal and derive equal benefits. So it is clear that political system is stressed and there is serious *crisis of confidence* in America similarly like in Europe.

There are two distinct power-centre in the world, "U.S.A and its allies Japan and South-Korea and of course west-European countries on one side of the divide and the two giant countries **Russia** and **China** on other side of the divide and in between the two powerful block are the Islamists forces. While China is ostensibly creating massive problems for all its neighbouring countries, and expanding its territory by building and constructing artificial islands in South-China Sea (SCS), Chinese are viciously intimidating and threatening other countries in east-Asia as well to India, Chinese indulging in illegal fishing and allegedly drilling oil wells for oil & gas exploration in SCS, There is *Russian aggression* in east-Europe, Kremlin has allegedly destabilized **Ukraine** and it is alleged it wants to repeat the same in other neighbouring countries as well, it is alleged that Russians want to expand their territory, Russia is a big fish in the ocean and it wants to swallow all the small fish, audacious and belligerent Russian President **Vladimir Putin** alleged sly motive and plan is to revive 20th century Soviet Union, and wants to re-conquer the east-European countries and establish Russian rule, Putin allegedly wants to decimate the "European Union." Russia is a large and resource rich nation and massively armed with nuclear weapons, and China is an unprecedented and undisputed Economic power in the world, the largest economy with abundant cash resources and influence, so, the Islamists have already made their intention clear and have put the world on notice, that, they'll destroy everything that is un-Islamic and annihilate all those who refuse to pledge their allegiance to their beloved **prophet Muhammad**, and besides Islam both Russia and China have aggressive plan and ulterior motives enough to destroy the planet "earth" and humanity. On the other side the U.S.A. and all its allies and friendly nations are flabbergast, absolutely stunned and have no concrete plan or strategy to deal with situation that could at any point in time *spiral out of contro*l.

The frequent brutal assaults by terrorist groups owing allegiance to Islam with great degree of consistency, targeting innocent civilian population and killing mainly Non-Muslims, is all but obvious to spark anti-Muslim backlash, as it said, that, for every action there is a reaction, and for every reaction there is a counter reaction, so not surprising for brutal inhuman activities of several Islamist terrorist organizations it was obvious to have a retaliatory reaction and inevitable retribution, I've observed and it has been reported in media as well that Islamophobia reached all time high during 2015, anti-Islam sentiments all over from Russia to Europe to America, non-Islamic communities infuriated with acts of Muslim jihadists, their anger began to be felt, hate crimes against Muslims started increasing especially in Europe and in U.S., because majority of innocent people killed by jihadists are/were Europeans and Americans.

It is indeed worrisome for those folks who love to live in peace, as abrupt rise in islamophobia will bring further pain to humanity, because the Far-Right and Right-wing politicians and political parties are trying to take advantage of prevailing anti-

Islam sentiments, similar to what Adolf Hitler did when he made political capital in 1920s/30s by taking advantage of than prevailing Anti-Semitic and anti-Jewish sentiments in Europe particularly in Germany.

Similarly in 21st century, quick to take advantage of prevailing anti-Muslim sentiments are the extreme Far-Right and Rightist leaning right-wing politicians and political parties, in prominent European countries and in U.S.A, particularly after the Paris terror attacks and massacre in U.S. city of San Bernardino (both incident happen in 2015) the right-wing politicians determinedly in hyper active mood started delivering hard hitting spirited speeches. Political extremists takes opportunity to further polarize the political system and society, uses opportunity to divide people, now we all know the past history, what **Napoleon Bonaparte and Adolf Hitler** did, they were destructive elements and destroyed major part of Europe, so this are historic facts, ambitious and eager political extremist are hero's for small section of society whom a small but significantly strong section of society feels and believes he/she (political extremist or a rightist leaning politician) is a messiah and will save them from evil, but another large section of society considers political extremist as an opportunist politician and a monster.

France, Britain, Russia and U.S. are all heavily nuclear armed nations, **wrong person for a right job**, if in modern times, an extremist hothead person in any of these nuclear armed country succeeds in occupying highest political office, becomes President or Prime-minister of any one of these country or in more than one of these countries, with his or her fingers on nuclear button, such an irresponsible frivolous person could create a havoc, and potentially destroy humanity.

Therefore, Islam in itself is dangerous evil, but, Islamophobia is even bigger and more devastating evil. Distinct dislike for Islam and Islamic people by majority of non-Muslim population of our world, growing religious intolerance, frustration is an common emotional reaction, therefore in anger and disappointment in many countries systematically brainwashed people are recklessly helping evil of another type, and through electoral process in elections by voting for the so-called ultra nationalist political parties, people are conveniently handing political power to wrong person or persons.

I once overheard someone saying, "The entire human Civilization will collapse, if Oil Wells runs dry."

What is so significant about it? Why is petroleum crude oil & gas so important for us (humans)? Yes, indeed, it's very important, because your "Footwear, underwear and cookware" every wear and ware contains crude oil in it?

Whenever the topic for discussion is Crude oil & gas, one particular region of world and its people comes to everyone's mind, Yep, they are the Arabs, and the Persian Gulf and Arabian Peninsula region of the world.

Outside the Arab world most people have this popular misconception that because there is massive petroleum crude oil reserves in Middle-east Arabian countries, therefore by default every Arab citizen is Rich and wealthy, No that's not true, yes, there are many Arabs in the Mid-east Arabian countries who are exceptionally wealthy, but those folks who have wealth have got less to do with oil but more to do with their business acumen and skills, while many individual Arabs are rich because they are well connected with political hierarchy and have direct access to ruling political families, but significantly large percentage of population in countries like Iraq, Saudi Arabia, Yemen, Syria, Jordan and Egypt etc are economically backwards and considered poor, also historically the unemployment rate has stubbornly remain high in several Arabian countries, unemployment rate in many Arabian countries have for decades remain in higher Double-Digit."

One common question, which most people eagerly ask is, why do Western countries as well as Chinese and Japanese take keen interest in Persian Gulf and Arabian countries internal matters? Is it all because of Oil or are there some other interest and reasons attached? The answer is, not really Oil & Gas, its true in 1970s and 1990s the Western countries and Japanese were overwhelmingly dependent on supplies of Oil & gas from the Arab countries situated in the mid-east Asia, but equation changed because in the 21st century petroleum Oil & gas has been discovered in many other parts of the world, large reserves of oil and gas has been discovered and are being commercially exploited, between 2004 and 2013 many new petroleum oil and gas fields were discovered in many different parts of the world chiefly in countries in Central-Asia, Africa and South-America, but also the U.S.A the largest and biggest consumer of oil in the world has discovered huge quantity of oil and gas in its own backyard, new age modern technology called **"Fracking" to explore Shale Oil & Gas from deep under the surface by brutally cracking the Rocks** has helped U.S.A greatly in achieving energy self-sufficiency. Additional supplies of Crude Oil from many Non-Arab countries and also increase use of Biofuel and renewable energy in several countries, all combination of reasons have made U.S and European nations less concern and less dependent of Oil & gas supplies from Persian gulf countries.

In 1980s and 90s, the Arab countries use to have immense clout and use to often intimidate other alleged unfriendly non-abiding countries of dire consequences, and threaten to disrupt the supply of crude oil with an intention to sabotage their economy, the oil rich Arab countries no longer have leverage, and their influence has receded considerably, as there is enough oil & gas available from alternate sources.

This is very crucial because it provides us perspective of what **"Power of Money"** does and can do, how potent is power of money? Let us get understanding of it.

The U.S, West-European nations, Japanese and Chinese are not particularly interested in petroleum Oil from Arab countries, they take extreme and keen interest in Arab countries because it provides the western corporates large consumer market to sell their products and services, it is the money that many Arab countries earns from selling petroleum oil in international market is what matters most to the Americans, Europeans, Chinese and Japanese governments and their corporates, their businesses and companies sells everything to the Arab consumers, the Arabs buys Food items and Medicines, Automobiles and Aircrafts, Collection of Arts and Paintings, Fancy clothes and perfumes, arms and ammunition, fighter jets and ships.

For U.S and its allies (the west-Europeans and Japanese) on one side and the Chinese and Russians on the other side, what extravagantly matters most to both faction and sides is their business and commercial interest to gain enormous Business Profits, that's the absolute reason, why they take keen interest in the Persian and Arabian countries.

When a Person or a country have immense Power of Money, obviously they'll also have incredible Purchasing power to buy and to purchase many different items and products, so, when a Person or a country/countries or for that matter anyone and anybody who has/have solid Purchasing power, hence many people and business owners by choice or by compulsion will follow that particular Person/persons to sell them and to convince them to buy many different items and products. This is why "Power of Money" is the greatest Power a person or a country can have, and this is precisely the reason why so many people around the World so desperately needs money.

Money-money-money; money arguably is each humans top priority, few people in world have lots of money, but, lots of people in world have less money or no money.

The reasons why there's chaos and troubles in many Muslim ruled countries and in Muslim dominated countries, it is because of economic backwardness, with large Muslim population socially and economically backwards, in Muslim dominated countries like Afghanistan, Pakistan, Bangladesh, Tunisia, Egypt, Somalia and many more countries there is high level of unemployment and or underemployment, big majority of people find it difficult to find jobs, so people have less or no money in their pockets, but at the same time rising prices of essentials are increasing cost of living, day to day expenses are rising but earning opportunities are dwindling.

Religion holds back progress, who has failed whom? "Has their religion (Islam) failed Muslims or Muslim folks have failed their religion?" it is their religion (Islam) that has failed Muslims.

Backwardness no development, no new industrial projects, no plan of new business investments, all is not well in Muslim ruled countries, millions of Muslim families living and surviving in desperate poverty, can't simply blame terrorism and corruption for all the failures in many Muslim ruled countries.

Muslim folks loyalty is only with their religion and not with humanity, people live life to serve purpose of their religion and care less to serve purpose of humanity, callous and arrogant Muslim community but particularly the Sunni Muslim community without any remorse and regrets publically calls every Non- Sunni Muslim religious communities and people as Kafir (infidels) and considers infidels as evil, and Sunni Muslims are of the view that harming infidels in any which manner is their mandated holy duty, Sunnis endeavour is to have this world free of Kafirs (infidels) by any which means possible.

Secular peace loving and liberals considers jihadists elements as terrorists and monsters, but for the Sunni Muslim community those members of their community who joins jihadists group and becomes a jihadi, the Jihadists are considered sacred and for Sunnis whosoever is a jihadi is part of Islamic army and duty of Islamic army is to wipe out all those people and everything in world that is non-Islamic.

It is often debated and discussed at length in public places as well in media, that it is oil money that is funding and aiding Sunni jihadist forces, many political analysts blame and accuses the wealthy oil rich Sunni Arab countries like the Saudis, Qataris and Kuwaitis for funding and financing Sunni extremism and terrorism, it is alleged that most of the Islamic schools and institutions in many different countries are funded by wealthy oil rich Arab countries, and Islamic schools and institutions are perfect breeding ground for radicalization process, young boys and girls are brainwashed, are incited and encouraged to take up Guns and Explosive materials in their hands and do not show any remorse and not to hesitate one bit firing and blasting Non-Sunni Muslim people anywhere in the world so as to fulfil their beloved prophet dream and Islamic god "Allah's" order to establish complete Islamic rule all over the world.

Many medieval Muslim thinkers, overwhelmingly pursue strong Islamist agenda, in mostly Muslim dominated countries young Sunni Muslim boys and girls are prevented from pursuing modern era graduate studies and university studies, schools and institutions in few of the Islamic countries are often brutally attacked, schools and universities in Pakistani city of Peshawar often comes under attack, terrorists brutally killing teachers and students inside schools and universities classrooms.

Insular belief and mind-set as well as rigid attitude, large population not willing to change with times are some of the uncanny reasons for social and economic backwardness and also for political instability in many Muslim countries.

Massive fall in prices of petroleum oil and gas since the middle of year 2014, some political analysts thought and felt will help dent Islamic terrorism because the large oil and gas producing Sunni Arab countries will earn lot less money, crude oil prices falling from the high of $115 per barrel in first half of 2014 to as low as $28 per barrel in January-2016, but on the contrary the Sunni militants and terrorists attacks and activities further increased since 2014, Sunni terrorists vigorously have been targeting and attacking non-Sunni Muslim targets around the world.

Steepest fall in oil prices, oil and gas producing Arab nations are in quandary, because of escalating violence and civil wars in many Islamic countries also because of Islamic sectarian strife, it is difficult to ascertain the fact as in due to massive drop in oil prices if the once cash rich Arabs still have cash dollars in hands or not, whatsoever maybe the truth about Arab's finances, but one thing is evident that due to major disturbance and increased terrorism in Islamic world, the cash rich Arab countries like Saudi Arabia, Qatar and Kuwait are forced to increase their defence budget, squeeze on resources, the Sunni Arab countries but also Shia ruled Iraq have to spend more money buying arms and ammunitions, sharp increases in defence expenditure, all this means that Arabs are earning lot less money but have to spend lot more money on buying arms, food and medicines, plus at same time they also have to take care of their respective country's citizens social security and welfare.

Disastrous fall in prices of petroleum oil and gas has or will force countries like Iraq and Saudi Arabia to borrow more money from international financial markets to finance their increase expenditure, which will increase Arab countries sovereign debt and if oil prices sustains lower levels for longer period of time, in which case all Arab countries will have to drastically reduce subsidies and cut benefits that they've long been providing their citizens and will be compel to raise local taxes, this is fearful situation an imminent risk that increase in taxes on citizens and massive cut in subsidies will further jeopardize the Islamic world and cause more civilian unrest and create political instability. Also because in good times these wealthy Sunni Arab countries Saudi Arabia, Qatar, Kuwait provides large financial aid and grants and financial support to many impoverish Sunni Muslim dominated countries like Pakistan, Bangladesh and North-Sudan etc, if oil revenue falls and income declines in which case Arabs won't be in position to provide prodigious financial support to other chiefly Sunni Muslim countries and will be unable fund various social and religious Islamic institutions.

There are dual effects felt for everything that's substantive, the stronger you become the more vulnerable you are, when an individual person or be it a country, becomes rich and wealthy, the power of wealth makes a person or the country's ruling administration restless and insane, on the other side poverty as well makes person/persons or a country increasingly frustrated and feeble, so, being influential rich and wealthy, or, being poor and stricken, both types of situation are dangerous; This is what has happen or is happening with **Islam**, as, Islam the religion and the follower of Islam have for long been of delusional view that they are incredibly strong force and that they have sufficient muscle and money power to take over the whole world, by all means at their disposal. The real problem is which seemingly have created bigger problems for the world as well is that, Islam and its followers the Muslims have made tremendous fundamental mistake in overestimating their ability and capacity to destroy everything that is non-Islamic in this world, and even bigger blunder the Islamic folks have made is that they gravely underestimated the striking capacity and financial strength and power of non-Islamic communities,

The firm belief among Muslim is, if the entire Sunni Islam unites, then they can certainly achieve their objective of establishing Islamic caliphate all over the world and that no one can stop them from conquering the whole world. Precisely this is the reason that almost every-day you listen the Islamic clerics and jihadist terrorists threatening the world's non-Muslim population of dire consequences if any one dares to become obstacle.

The unfounded belief of Islamic folks, has made the entire Sunni-Muslim community arrogant and their overconfidence has made them more vulnerable, Muslim brothers and sisters are wasting huge financial resources and human lives.

Muslims have brazen double standards, while Sunni-Muslims mince no words in condemning and mocking the entire non-Muslim population and without any regret or shame calls every non-Sunni Muslim communities and those people who do not believe in Islamist doctrine as **Kafir** (infidels), an according to Islamic doctrine Kafirs (infidels) are evil worshippers, and according to hardline Islamist belief harming and punishing or even going to an extent of killing the infidels is considered as holy duty of every practicing devout Muslim, Muslim clerics and priests on record preach and advices to followers of Islam that everything that is produced by non-Islamic communities or atheists (unbelievers) is Haraam (illegitimate), hence Muslims should restrain themselves from using and consuming foods items and many other consumer products and material that are produced by Pagan, Jewish and other non-believers of Islam.

You may listen such slogans in most of the Islamic countries as well in Muslim dominated countries and localities, Muslims shouting death to America, boycott Israel, Muslims are severely critical towards Jewish community, and also we hear from Muslims many other slogans condemning non-Muslims and idol worshippers, but, members of Muslim communities and followers of Islam when they are wounded and injured or suffering from illness to heal their wounds and to cure diseases they consume medicines which apparently are researched and developed by Jewish scientists, and manufactured in Jewish or Pagan (idol and nature worshipers) owned factories. Muslims makes extensive use of scientific technologies which again are researched, design and developed by Jewish or atheists and most likely manufactured in Jewish or Christian owned factories.

Similarly Islamic countries and Muslim institutions graciously accept economic and financial aid and help from non-Islamic countries governments (U.S.A., Japan and European governments provides Billions of Dollars in economic aid and other incentives to so many Islamic and Muslim dominated countries) and financial institutions, so accepting money and donations from financial institutions which are controlled by Jewish or atheists is OK for Muslim folks, seeking asylum and refuge in non-Islamic country is OK, but, yet Muslims are not ready to concede, they continue pouring stream of invective against non-Sunni Muslim communities, Muslims will take money, accept economic aid packages from non-Muslim governments and institutions and use their technology and consume medicines, yet Muslims brazenly calls non-Muslim communities "Kafir" (infidel) and vociferate for total destruction of unbelievers or to say they (Sunni-Muslims) vows to eliminate anyone and everything that is non-Islamic.

Extremely clever, cunning and crafty is how I would describe the Islamic jihadi army hierarchy or bosses whosoever these mysterious people are, the strategy of the Jihadis or to say Islamist army is to traumatize the world's non-Sunni Muslim population, instead of challenging rival enemies army in open battle field for full frontal confrontation and for decisive outcome, they've adopted more subtle combative strategy, efficiently fighting low key war, the Sunni jihadists and terrorist groups by frequently targeting and attacking non-Sunni Muslim population whenever and wherever in so many different parts of the world, it proves more cost effective and above all more damaging and harming. Sporadic terror attacks at strategic locations exerts tremendous psychological pressure on non-Muslim countries governments as well on common-people.

Islamic sectarian strife, wars in Islamic countries, poverty in Muslim dominated Asian and African countries, all these combination of reasons creates more humanitarian reason and excuse for Muslims to migrate and populate European and American countries. Here is another perspective, the Islamic jihadi forces and terrorists in 18th, 19th and 20th century have firmly consolidated its position and have strengthen its bases in much of Asian and African continents, it seems obvious in 21st century Islamist Jihadists are prying to takeover European continent, the allege strategy of Islamic jihadists commanders would be to terrorize the mainstream European society, sporadic deadly terror attacks hitting prominent European towns and cities, would potentially severely hurt Europe's economy, create fear in minds of Europeans and cause sense of insecurity. Europeans seeing rise in Islamic numbers and increase in Muslim population inside Europe, feeling enormous pressure at least some of the frustrated Europeans will be *compel to leave Europe for good* and move to other safer destination outside European continent for safe and secured life, this is precisely what the Islamic Jihadi army commanders would like the most because that's exactly what they would want to happen, as it will increase Muslim population and decrease European population, after all politics is all about numbers, with rise in Muslim population it will make Sunni-Muslims task easier to gain total and comprehensive control of Europe.

Something similar happened in Africa, when Muslims were systematically gaining control of many African countries, the non-Muslim Black people under duress and frustration moved out of Africa and migrated to countries in Europe or America.

Again the same question arises; Does "Petro-dollars" funds Islamic terrorism and extremism? Western media and politicians for decades have been complaining that the wealthy oil rich Sunni Arab countries such as Saudi Arabia, Qatar and Kuwait have been promoting and generously funding Islamic extremism and terrorism, so it is alleged that several prominent Muslim countries governments have been helping and promoting jihadist (Islamic holy-warriors) groups. It maybe be perception of many but perhaps not a reality. Perhaps, I would say its partially true that couple of Sunni Arab countries earning large amount of money selling petroleum oil & gas uses some amount of the oil income to fund Islamic extremism and terrorism, but as it is that no criminal gang or terrorist group can possibly sustain itself unless they've political patronage and until such time that they enjoy support of particular dominant ethnic or religious community. Therefore Sunni jihadist terrorism can't survive for a moment more unless they are backed and aided by their community members, clerics and political leaders.

There is a perception, and also true, can't deny the fact that there is **State sponsor terrorism**, wherein government of particular country for strategic reasons and for larger interest and benefit of their country they do finance extremist and terrorist groups, but it is equally true the other way around as well, which is that many criminal gangs and terrorist groups as well supports States by providing financial and other material help to governments and contributes significant amount of money for the welfare of people belonging to their own religious community.

Terrorism have been institutionalized, criminal syndicates and cartels as well as terrorist groups mobilize resources and finances from many different ways and means, Crime and Corruption have unofficially gained <u>Industry Status</u>. So talking about Islamic extremism and terrorism, Islamic terror and criminal enterprises, gangs and syndicates earns money and generates cash from many different means and are in position to fund governments and give big political donations to influential political leaders and political parties.

Sunni jihadist groups like "ISIS, Al Qaeda, Al Shabaab, Boko Haram," and many more fringe terror groups are allegedly involved in many illicit business and trade, while Africa based terror groups like Al Shabaab and Boko Haram, earns big amount of money to fund their jihadist project mainly through Poaching and killing wildlife in African forest and jungles and trade in endanger animals skins, bones and ivory, also earns money from illegal mining of minerals and extortion, seeking donations forcing people to donate money for Islamic causes which obviously is for jihad (Islam holy-war).

Similarly other terrorist groups like ISIS, Al Qaeda and Taliban and other criminal gangs mostly operating in west-Asia's Arabian countries, Afghanistan and Pakistan are allegedly involve in many unlawful and illegal business and trade such as "human trafficking, drug trafficking, trafficking in human organs, fake currency, counterfeit medicines, cybercrime, gambling and illegal betting and match fixing." So reverse is true as well with hundreds of billions of dollars they earn from all kinds of illicit and illegal business and trade, many of the criminal gangs and terrorist groups finance and funds also bribes the governments and government officials of many countries.

When topic of discussion is Islamic terrorism, one name that comes in minds of many of us and that name is **Osama Bin Laden**, Laden the allege founder of terror group <u>Al Qaeda</u> who became symbol of Sunni Islam jihad. Decades after the collapse of great **Ottoman Empire** in 1918/19 after the end of WWI, apparently it was Osama Laden who in 21st century revived struggle for establishing **Sunni Islam Caliphate** which means Sunni-Islam rule the world over. Especially in western world in Europe and America people know Osama bin laden as dreaded jihadist or terrorist, but wait a moment there is another man seriously associated with global Islamic jihad and he is a phenomenon in crime world and his name is **Dawood Ibrahim** who perhaps is more rich and resourceful than Osama bin laden was, Dawood Ibrahim an Indian born most prolific and high-profile international criminal, Dawood fled India in mid-1980s because for the brutal crimes he had committed hence he was wanted in many criminal cases, so as to avoid his arrest and he also feared of him being killed by rival criminal gangs so he left India and since than established his base in Dubai and Pakistani port city of Karachi.

Dawood Ibrahim arguably the most successful and influential gangster extremely wealthy and powerful who is supposedly worth billions of dollars, a very popular person enjoys celebrity status in south and west-Asia, **The Don** or **Bhai** (Brother) as he is popularly called and his criminal gang known as **D-Company**, Dawood Ibrahim's allege illegal business interest are "Contract killings, illegal betting and match fixing, drug trafficking, fake currency and financing Bollywood (Hindi films) movies and distribution," and many more illicit businesses and criminal activities deeply rooted throughout the world. Money earned by Dawood Ibrahim through criminal activities are then through frontend companies invested in many other mainstream businesses like Hotels, airlines, properties and stock-markets. It is alleged that Dawood is a principle financer of various Islamic terrorist groups largely operating in Pakistan and Afghanistan and when in need many Muslim nation governments in south-Asia and west-Asia seeks financial help from Dawood.

Dawood Ibrahim may have fled India to never possibly return back, but his heart remains in country of his birth, majority population in Indian sub-continent countries and in west-Asia passionately love watching Bollywood films (Hindi movies) and take keen interest in playing and watching their favourite sport **Cricket**, so does Dawood Ibrahim as well have great love and passion for Cricket and it is primarily through Cricket and Bollywood film industry Dawood has maintain close link with India and his compatriots, Dawood also have serious business interest in India as well because many of his close friends and business associates as well his siblings and relatives are living in India, Dawood Ibrahim allegedly pays generous amount of money to Indian politicians and bureaucrats and he finances election campaigns of many prominent Indian political parties. So in all not only Osama bin laden, but Dawood Ibrahim as well is a master strategist, clever and shrewd good at manoeuvring business deals, he's a prominent personality working and helping insensitive cause of his religion Sunni-Islam,

To define Islam and its followers the Muslims, the critics and opponents of Islam describe "Islam is brutal religion and thoroughly chaotic," the sympathizers and supporters of Islam says "Islam is humble and peaceful religion," people are free to say and speak "what they feel and like."

But as we unbiasedly assess Islam, it is so that, "Muslims ruthlessly harm others and creates problems for others (non-Muslims)," also true is "Muslims harms fellow Muslims and creates more problems for themselves and for their communities," talking about growing violence world over, Islamist terrorists killing innocent people, true as it is evident, but there's another bigger perspective, just think again, Islamic extremists and terrorists kills and harm more Muslims than anyone else, yes maximum victims of brutal Islamic terrorism are their own "Muslims," Sunni jihadists and also Islamic countries official army and security forces not only kills more Muslims but they also destroy livelihood of Millions of Muslims.

Islam is religion brutally divided into two faction "**Shia** and **Sunni**," and it will be worth noting that all terribly inhuman and devastatingly dangerous terrorist groups such as "ISIS, Al Qaeda, Boko Haram, Taliban, Al Shabaab" and so many more such jihadi groups owe their allegiance to Sunni Islam, Islamic terrorism is culture of Sunni Islam.

There are many perspective but bigger perspective is religion, there is too much confusion in minds of many as to whether or not all three supposedly Abrahamic religions Judaism, Christianity and Islam follows the same god, a very crucial but always a controversial topic to debate, devout followers of Islam's unfounded beliefs, stubborn as they (Muslims) are not establishing the truth of their religion.

Muslim people are thoroughly misinformed and seriously misguided by astute Muslim clerics and priests, using unprecedented tactics to systematically brainwash the Muslim population and to entice and encourage the gullible non-Muslims to embrace Islam and force them to pledge allegiance to their beloved

Prophet Muhammad, the Muslim clerics and priests preaches the alleged message of their prophet to the followers of Islam, they in their discourse and sermons says, **"There is only one God and that god is Allah, you (Muslims) who follow Islam are the best creatures of Allah (Islamic God), and Allah loves you all and the remaining non-believers are Kafir (Infidels), and with regards to Infidels -- Muslims are thought to believe that God made serious mistake in creating non-Islamic religious communities therefore they (people who do not follow Sunni-Islam) are flawed and worse creatures hence they will burn in fire of Hell, so they (Islamic clerics) preach and assures Muslims that "Paradise for Sunni-Muslims and fire of hell for non-Muslims."**

There is it seems a deliberate attempt to polarize global civil society and to divide world's population on religious and cultural lines, the Sunni-Muslim population world over as of 2016 is approximately 1.2 Billion, with Sunni Islam on one side of the divide and the rest on the other side and leave nothing in between, so, this is why I say **"Islam versus the rest."** Islam have nothing much to lose so they are not losing much, by creating nightmarish and chaotic situation for non-Sunni Muslim population all over the world, Islam only have something to gain so they are gaining a lot (economic and political power).

With major parts and large territories in Asia and Africa already under Islamic control, all eyes are on what will be the next move of the Islamists in Europe! Will Islam succeed in conquering Europe? And if Islam by any chance does succeed in its plan of capturing political power in Europe than sky will be the limit, Islam will then rule the world. Or, will **Islam implode**? What if the Islamic people themselves destroy Islam?

The Muslim institutions and religious council hierarchy, clerics and politicians for generations have successfully indoctrinated minds of naïve and gullible individuals; here in an interesting article to have better and scientific perspective of who Allah (the Muslim God) actually is and what is its significance Article title **"Allah – The Moon God" The Archeology of the Middle East**"- "The religion of Islam has as its focus of worship a deity by the name of *"Allah."* The Muslims claim that Allah in pre-Islamic times was the biblical God of the Patriarchs, prophets, and apostles. The issue is thus one of continuity. Was *"Allah"* the biblical God or a pagan god in Arabia during pre-Islamic times? The Muslim's claim of continuity is essential to their attempt to convert Jews and Christians for if *"Allah"* is part of the flow of divine revelation in Scripture, then it is the next step in biblical religion. Thus we should all become Muslims. But, on the other hand, if Allah was a pre-Islamic pagan deity, then its core claim is refuted. Religious claims often fall before the results of hard sciences such as archeology. We can endlessly speculate about the past or go and dig it up and see what the evidence reveals. This is the only way to find out the truth concerning the origins of Allah. As we shall see, the hard evidence demonstrates that the god Allah was a pagan deity. In fact, he was the Moon-god who was married to the sun goddess and the stars were his daughters.

Archaeologists have uncovered temples to the Moon-god throughout the Middle East. From the mountains of Turkey to the banks of the Nile, the most wide-spread religion of the ancient world was the worship of the Moon-god. In the first literate civilization, the Sumerians have left us thousands of clay tablets in which they described their religious beliefs. As demonstrated by Sjoberg and Hall, the ancient Sumerians worshipped a Moon-god who was called many different names. The most popular names were Nanna, Suen and Asimbabbar. His symbol was the crescent moon. Given the amount of artifacts concerning the worship of this Moon-god, it is clear that this was the dominant religion in Sumeria. The cult of the Moon-god was the most popular religion throughout ancient Mesopotamia. The Assyrians, Babylonians, and the Akkadians took the word Suen and transformed it into the word Sin as their favorite name for the Moon-God. As Prof. Potts pointed out, *"Sin is a name essentially Sumerian in origin which had been borrowed by the Semites."*

In ancient Syria and Canna, the Moon-god Sin was usually represented by the moon in its crescent phase. At times the full moon was placed inside the crescent moon to emphasize all the phases of the moon. The sun-goddess was the wife of Sin and the stars were their daughters. For example, Istar was a daughter of Sin. Sacrifices to the Moon-god are described in the Pas Shamra texts. In the Ugaritic texts, the Moon-god was sometimes called Kusuh. In Persia, as well as in Egypt, the Moon-god is depicted on wall murals and on the heads of statues. He was the Judge of men and gods. The Old Testament constantly rebuked the worship of the Moon-god (Deuteronomy 4:19; 17:3; II Kings 21:3, 5; 23:5; Jeremiah 8:2; 19:13; Zephaniah 1:5, etc.) When Israel fell into idolatry, it was usually the cult of the Moon-god. As a matter of fact, everywhere in the ancient world, the symbol of the crescent moon can be found on seal impressions, steles, pottery, amulets, clay tablets, cylinders, weights, earrings, necklaces, wall murals, etc. In Tell-el-Obeid, a copper calf was found with a crescent moon on its forehead. An idol with the body of a bull and the head of man has a crescent moon inlaid on its forehead with shells. In Ur, the Stele of Ur-Nammu has the crescent symbol placed at the top of the register of gods because the Moon-god was the head of the gods. Even bread was baked in the form of a crescent as an act of devotion to the Moon-god. The Ur of the Chaldees was so devoted to the Moon-god that it was sometimes called Nannar in tablets from that time period.

A temple of the Moon-god has been excavated in Ur by Sir Leonard Woolley. He dug up many examples of moon worship in Ur and these are displayed in the British Museum to this day. Harran was likewise noted for its devotion to the Moon-god. In the 1950's a major temple to the Moon-god was excavated at Hazer in Palestine. Two idols of the Moon god were found. Each was a stature of a man sitting upon a throne with a crescent moon carved on his chest. The accompanying inscriptions make it clear that these were idols of the Moon-god. Several smaller statues were also found which were identified by their inscriptions as the "daughters" of the Moon-god. What about Arabia? As pointed out by Prof. Coon, *"Muslims are notoriously loath to preserve traditions of earlier paganism and like to garble what pre-Islamic history they permit to survive in anachronistic terms."*............

Touching base with extreme realities of the so-called Abrahamic religions, when we talk of Islam, we always talk of its founder Muhammad, the so-called alleged last prophet of God "Muhammad" is discussed extensively, but, no one really discusses, as in, how Islam was formed? What made Muhammad so great and achieve unprecedented success? All talks of god sending his angel "**Gabriel**" down on earth to communique his message to Muhammad, and so many such imaginative and false stories, unscientific explanation and narratives that we listen and read, but these are all wild imagination and rubbish talks, no secular scholars and intellectuals will ever believe such nonsense theories and stories.

Here is a real true perspective in brief to understand "*how Islam came into being, and, what and who made Muhammad so popular and powerful person ever born on this planet,*" > Muhammad was born into low-income family in either Mecca or Medina modern day part of Saudi Arabia, he belonged to Banu Hashim clan which was part of Quraysh tribe a very powerful tribe in Medina, Muhammad remained unmarried single till he was 25years of age, he use to survive well doing odd job and business deals, even though Muhammad was an absolute illiterate, but it has been written about him that he had excellent oratory and negotiating skills, as it is said that "behind every successful man there is a woman," according to historians have recorded that in 595CE, he married **Khadīja bint Khuwaylid** and she apparently was 15 years older in age than him.

Khadija was also from same Quraysh tribe and was a successful businesswoman, she was a merchant and use to trade large consignment of goods and products, because of her business success she was very influential and respected throughout Arabian region, Khadija was rich, she had staggering personality was shrewd, intelligent, smart, compassionate, use to help and support many people, she was kind and generous woman, but, she did not believe and did not like worshipping idols, but she in her house use to have idol of **Al-Uzza**, "(**Al-'Uzzá** was one of the three chief goddesses of Arabian religion in pre-Islamic times and was worshiped by the pre-Islamic Arabs along with **Allāt** and **Manāt**)," so it was Muhammad's first wife Khadija significantly guided and helped Muhammad gain success, Islam is basically brainchild NOT OF Muhammad's but his first wife Khadija, Khadija was the first person to embrace Islam and she is the one who promoted him as prophet of the believers.

It so happened that during 6th and 7th century people of Arabia and Mesopotamia were fed-up of frequent wars and violence between various kingdoms and warlords, chaotic situation in the Arabian region, "poverty, persecution, high inflation and unemployment," had made people in the region restless as they were feeling insecure, the people wanted peace and a leader to lead them, and Muhammad's first wife being a successful businesswoman having trading business spread across Arabian and Mesopotamia region, hence she was well connected had good contacts in the region, her sources use to constantly update her with information regarding economic and political situation, she was widely travelled and intelligent woman, knew all about peoples aspiration and what is the mood of the people in Arabia and Mesopotamia region, when Khadija realized that people are disenchanted with the political leaders and kings who rule them, she seized an opportunity to exploit the than existing ground situation, and the generous woman that she (Khadija) was, instead of promoting herself and becoming leader and chieftain herself, she used all her resources and the goodwill she had among large majority of people for all her philanthropic work and help she had rendered to so many people, she used it all to her advantage and promoted her husband, she promoted Muhammad as prophet of the believers, and sometime in 610CE launched a peoples movement and named it **Islam** headed by her doting husband Muhammad, Islam was initially a peaceful movement project, majority of people of Hejaz (present day -- Saudi Arabia) liked new peace initiative and gracefully accepted Muhammad as their new leader, many unconditionally pledged allegiance to Muhammad, so Islam was initially started as peaceful movement and had given people a new hope. Muhammad till the time his first wife Khadīja bint Khuwaylid was alive remained loyal to her and did not had any other wife/wives or any extramarital affairs.

"(It is not clear, as to, how many biological children Muhammad had of his own? But, Muhammad for sure had one child from his first wife Khadija bint Khuwaylid had a beautiful daughter her name '**Fatima-Zahra**,' like mother like daughter, Fatima was beautiful, kind-hearted, brave and courageous woman, she married Muhammad's cousin **Ali ibn Abi Talib**, when after death of Muhammad there was rebellion in Islam over his succession and leadership issue, Fatima along with her husband Imam Ali founded **Shiite Islam**, yes, Fatima is founder of Shia Islam, she is mother of the followers of Shia Islam, she had two sons **Imam Hassan** and

Imam Hussein; Fatima resolutely and vehemently opposed the Sunni caliph and Sunni-Islam terrorism).”

But sadly in 620CE Muhammad's first wife Khadija died, and after death of his first wife things dramatically began to change in Islam and unfortunately changed for the worse, till his first wife Khadija was alive Muhammad was disciplined and civilized person, was a very humble man, but soon after death of his first wife, Muhammad was corrupted, Muhammad started receiving advises from all the wrong people, Muhammad broke all his earlier promises and commitments he had made to people of Medina and Hejaz. Islam from peaceful movement became violent and corrupt, Islam became political movement and started attacking and looting villages and resorted to forceful conversions, in wars Islamic army started looting wealth and raping young women and girls, Muhammad himself became self-spoiled he started marrying one woman after another, some record suggest after death of his first wife Khadija, Muhammad married as many as **8** more women, most notable was his marriage to 6 year old kid the voracious **Aisha**, it has been said that he married Aisha when her age was 6 and consummated her when she was just 9 years old, apart from many wives Muhammad also had many concubines, Muhammad voraciously indulged in sex with many women, so initially as it was that Islam was a peaceful religion and its founder Muhammad was a humble man, but after the death of Muhammad's first wife Khadija neither Islam remained peaceful nor did Muhammad remained humble, it will be safe for us to assume "evil took control of both Islam and its founder **Muhammad.**”

One incident I would like mentioning to prove the so-called messenger of peace prophet Mohammed's (Allah's apostles) abhorrent attributes: in one of the many wars which Mohammed fought in 7th century to establish Islam "At the Massacre of Khaybar, Muhammad brutally tortured a Jewish chieftain for extracting information about where he had hidden his treasures. When the treasure was uncovered, the chieftain was beheaded. This chieftain was the husband of the most beautiful Jewish woman of Khaybar, the 17-year-old Safiyaah. Safiyaah's family members had been annihilated by Muhammad at the Banu Qurayza massacre. Now having beheaded her husband, the Prophet took Safiyah as his sex-slave and copulated on the same night." Another incident: "In the massacre of the Jewish Settlement of Bani Mustaliq, Muhammad captured their women and took twenty-year-old Jewish girl, Juwayriya as his sex-slave."

The followers of Islam should stop blaming others for their misery, the truth is that Islamic folks are inspired by all the wrong things in life, the Islamic doctrine and theology is failing the Muslims.

Between 2001 till 2016 as a result of <u>War on terror</u> and <u>Islamic religious wars</u> an estimated 2 million people have been killed or have died unnatural death due to terrorism related violence and social chaos due to hunger and poverty in mostly Islamic and Muslim dominated countries in west-Asia and other Muslim dominated Asian and African countries. Worst affected and brutally harmed are countries such as "Syria, Yemen, Somalia, Afghanistan, Pakistan and of course Iraq from where it all began first in 1991. Few other Islamic countries such as "Turkey, Libya and Egypt" are/were other major trouble spot, Libya almost a failed state total anarchy complete breakdown of economic and political system, while Egypt and Turkey experienced increase in terror activities and massive rise in killings.

Islamists arrogance is responsible for so much bloodbath all over the world, who has failed whom' did the people followers of Islam failed their religion (Islam)? Or, has the religion (Islam) have failed its followers (people who follow Islam)? It is the latter, their religion "Islam" that has failed its followers, because the **documented constitution** of Islam and its core value is violent and preaches hatred instead of uniting it teaches to practice division, Islamists firmly believes that Islam is the best and supreme religion than compare to every other religion and their determined belief that Islamists are privilege people hence being born a Muslim makes them superior in every aspect and that followers of all other religions and or unbelievers are ugly creation of god so they are inferior and that non-Muslims are not worth calling humans worse than dogs and cats hence are

infidels and infidels are equal to evil therefore harming or even going as far as to killing the infidels is considered as holy duty of each Muslim and that's why these ill-conceived jihadists (holy warrior) are so resolutely out in open to eliminate all the non-Sunni Muslim population across the world. But is the approach and is it the right strategy to counter Islamic extremism and stop the menace of Jihadists killings of non-Muslims therefore in retaliation attack the Jihadists in their strong hold in Islamic countries where they are hiding and operating from.

American, Russian, French and also British army targeting the Jihadists or to say Islamic terrorists camps in Islamic countries resorting to blasting bombs, aerial bombardments, indiscriminate firing missiles and bullets on pretext of eliminating the terrorists, since these jihadists and terrorists hide and are provided shelter in towns and cities and blended among civilian population therefore frequent attacks by American and Russian army results in deaths of many more people most of whom are civilians. Fighting "fire with fire," tit for tat strategy is false and flawed strategy highly unyielding and will never ever succeed in subduing the **Islamic jihadi project**, in fact the more the western and Russian army attacks Muslim dominated areas and more killing only helps the jihadists cause as it encourages more Muslim youths to fight **jihad** (Islam' religious holy war) against the enemy (from Muslims perspective all those people in this world who do not pledge their allegiance to their prophet Muhammad and do not believe in Allah are considered as enemy of Islam). This is precise reason as to why *War on terror* has failed and instead Islam has become more stronger because the more the killings of Muslims it polarizes the society and divides world's population, so even more non-Muslim leftist leaning people come out in open and supports Islam.

Human lives matter, no matter what religion you follow or do not follow any religion, regardless of your ethnicity or skin colour, killing of people is never justifiable, be it a member of mainstream official army or a terrorist, we all after all are humans, whether it is Muslim jihadis who kills non-Muslims or the non-Muslim security forces in retaliation kills jihadists or by default other unarmed Muslims, no matter who dies it has to be construed as crime against humanity, we are all humans, human lives matter, therefore in retaliation to jihadists terror attacks > attacking Muslim dominated areas is not a good strategy, but than if a large section of world's population is flawed and behaving like an **evil** who wants to destroy humanity we can't keep silence and do nothing, here is a solution "similarly like economic and trade and diplomatic sanctions are impose on a country that flouts international rules creates problems for other countries and whose government is brutal dictatorial and harms and supresses their people and also pose threat to other countries around the world, like for example all kinds of punitive economic and diplomatic sanctions are impose on North-Korea for its allege role in harming world's peace, stringent sanctions were impose on Iran for its allege Nuclear programme and so many more countries including Russia have experienced sanctions in history and also in present times," similarly to subjugate and to neutralize the power of Islam and to thrash its arrogance for that the non-Sunni Muslim population the powerful American, Russian and European countries should **impose strict economic and diplomatic sanctions on Islam and on Islamists**, social boycott of Muslims till such time they disband their barbaric religious Islamic doctrine and stop treating other non-Muslims like 2nd grade inferior citizens, this is the only way to defeat the Islamists, a most honourable and effective strategy which will be absolutely eco-friendly, no violence and no killings, what more it will be absolutely cost free no money will be spent and problem is sorted out *once and for all*, Islamists will never ever dare to challenge the non-Muslim population of the world and will be force to respect humanity will learn to respect people of every other religion and the unbelievers.

If there are problems there are solutions but who is ready and willing to work to solve most pressing human problems, people in this world are inspired by all the wrong things that's why with false impression and faulty ideas in their mind they practice all the wrong things which works against humanity and have deadly consequences. Don't wait for others to take the first step, have a positive and determined approach towards life, you be the first to do things and show it to the world --- yes' it works, yes it makes the difference and brings about change for the betterment.

In the catastrophic or accidental view of history we are led to believe that historical events, such as wars and revolutions were the direct result of some sudden or surprising event. While the catastrophic view is accurate for weather, volcanoes and earthquakes, it does not always provide a realistic view of humanity and events influenced by man. We believe that current world events are not simply circumstantial, but the result of an organized campaign by an elite group of unseen and widely unknown world leaders. Their goal is to exercise absolute dictatorial control over the world, to establish a **New World Order.**

It is better to walk alone rather than walk with the crowd who are all walking in the wrong direction.

Be good to others, expect others to be good to you.

Man has/have created Religion and Religion has not created man. Religion is a man-made device designed to focus people's attention and energy on a single unchanging and uncompromising supreme being.

Religions survives because of People, but, People do not survive because of religions. As it said "Nature don't need people," it is "we People' who need Nature" for our survival, similarly it is the religions which need people for their survival and we people do not need religion or religions for our survival!

Who created whom? Humans created God a figment of our imagination or god created human beings.

People throughout history have created a god to meet their own needs and circumstances. But, the REAL God of the Universe cannot be the creation of mere man's logic and mental comprehension.

We are not "God," but our desire to be such takes us to madness.

Majority among us (humans) waste invaluable time of ours in our life time, thinking about God, talking about God, discussing about God, promoting god, defending god, gosh' so much god, most of the people we talk too, they use the word "**God**" as many time as they can possibly use during the course of the conversation, these devout religious people start conversation with the name of "God" and ends the conversation with the name of "God." Around the world many people spend unprecedented amount of their time in their life-time "thinking, talking, reading and understanding of or about <u>God</u>," so much time of theirs in their life-time is invested in God that they fail to understand their own-selves, such people who devout lot of their time and energy for religious purpose and in thinking and talking about god, apparently have less confidence in themselves and it invariably makes them less productive.

So much misleading information with regards to gods and goddesses, disinformation campaign by vested interest that **saints** and **angels** will perform miracles and will defeat the evil and cure diseases and will help bring incredible economic gain to you, people around the world waste enormously valuable time of their own practicing religious rituals and reading the so-called religious holy books, which are nothing but full of contradictions, unscientific narratives, vague and some laughable stories of divine healing super-natural power of god and falsely described and highly exaggerated events.

Do we really need religion/religions? Can't we humans survive without a religion? What are religions there for? Each damn religion preaches that their religion is the most authentic religion and best way to move closer to seek "Divine Blessings," they (priests and clerics) will always say to their followers that ours is the best religion and all other religions and religious beliefs are blunt, every religion claims that their religion is best and more holy compare to every other religions, such perception and conviction, well, I would say, it is indeed very scary, each people think their religion is superior than every other religions, it is because generation after generation parents and grandparents indoctrinates the minds of their children with religious thoughts and preaches them about supernatural power that their alleged God or Prophet possesses, it is so because people are not ready to open their mind and try to establish the truth "if at all there exist any element such as "God." Religion is one of the most sensitive issues and, although every religion encourages the idea of peace and tolerance, almost no one remains in peace or tolerates anything when it comes to their religion. History is full of **religious wars** and some of them have continued for years and killed **many**.

To my mind, Religion is a tool to manipulate mankind, religion and religious beliefs takes over full control over the minds of great masses.

Various religious institutions uses brainwashing, mind control, oppression, false teaching, guilt, shame, peer pressure and other bondage techniques to control members of their Sect and religious community, the underlying agenda of religious institution is desire to obtain power control and money.

The power to manipulate beliefs is all that matters most, because we humans live with beliefs and it is always easy to manipulate beliefs.

Flawed and reckless economic policies causes excruciating and irreparable damage to both social structure in civil society as well it severely harms the natural environment and ecological system. Whether we talk about the Chinese or Americans or the European Union countries Economic Policies which they have adopted in the 21st century is far from satisfactory, irresponsibly planned insensitive business and economic policies has resulted in causing major social problems and have created gender inequality besides it has increased discrimination and hatred crimes in civil societies. The gap between the rich and poor has widen substantially. The uncertain times have become even more uncertain, the reckless **printing of money** or to say frequent dose of economic stimulus package by the prominent industrialized nations like U.SA, Japan, China and Europe to boost their flagging economies after the infamous 2008 financial meltdown, lack of creative ideas and thoughts, instead the **Central Bankers** of prominent countries have found simple and easy way out that is to print unprecedented amount of Cash-currency notes for the purpose of creating artificially high cash liquidity in the banking system and tempt businesses and common-people to borrow more money for spending on buying consumer goods and to spend money on other extraordinary purchases.

The increase demand for industrial goods creates incessant demand for minerals and petroleum crude oil, and to meet rising demand for oil & gas, new technology has been invented in the 21st century called fracking to produce **Shale Oil**, the fracking technology that brutally cracks the rocks beneath the surface of the earth to pump out crude oil and gas, outrageously environment unfriendly fracking technology has caused profound harm to the environment, over mining digging the surface of the Earth deeper and deeper to extract minerals and pumping out crude oil has destroyed global environment and has dangerously unbalanced the ecological system, the weather and climatic condition around the globe is becoming more and more erratic and dreadful, due to which the world is experiencing frequent brutal natural disasters, causing unprecedented loses to public lives, properties and livelihood.

The **magic-stick** in 21st century to spur Economic growth is to create unprecedented amount of *cash liquidity* into the banking system, the **Central bankers** as a first step will reduced Key bank lending rate to 0%, if reducing interest rate to 0% fails to have desire impact on country's economic growth than the next measure Central bankers will announce stimulus economic package in which they'll print *Billions of dollars of cash-currency notes* for indefinite period of time and if that as well fails to spur economic growth and comprehensively fails to bring down ever so high unemployment rate, than, taking extreme step forward will reduce bank's key interest rate below 0%, that means **Negative interest rates**, so Negative interest-rate policy means the depositors instead of receiving interest income on the money they deposit with banks either earns no interest income or worst still the depositors have to pay banks interest or to say penalty per month to park their money with banks, those days are gone at least in leading industrialized nations, when people use to deposit their money and cash savings with banks and other government supported financial institutions and earn assured monthly interest income, or to say the **Fixed-income** market has been decimated, people are forced to take risk, common-people are lured and compelled to borrow more and spend more, which is extremely dangerous sign, Capitalists economic system has made stock-markets and commodity-markets a **casino**, people are left with little or no choice but to speculate on risky financial instruments and gamble with their money to earn money, such flawed and faulty economic policies as well are seriously responsible for increased crime and suicide rates around the world, also responsible for rising intolerance and hate crimes and religious extremism and terrorism.

Who is/are bigger and dangerous threat to the humanity? Who is actually destroying our **planet "earth"**? **Islamists terrorists** or the **Central bankers.** Islamic terrorism of course is serious problem but much more brutal and seriously harming humanity is reckless and irresponsible economic and monetary policies.

Talent is something we are born with and skills is something we learn, some people are intelligent and they realize what talent they have and accordingly learn appropriate skills, most individual people are naïve and they never realize the true hidden potential in them and remains laggards, lazybones people waste their talent, because they try doing all the wrong things in life which only adds to their misery, so timing is everything in life, and this is where many people lags big time, not ready to make right moves in life, not ready and willing to learn right things, always respect time, time is precious and time is mighty, time is money.

Those people who time their moves diligently and accurately always wins the race and succeed in life.

To be in business put others out of business, but, is it fair thing to do to destroy others happiness and livelihood? Again morality and ethics do not permit us to ruin others life and livelihood, but then in reality who cares, some people among us have more subdued and humble approach towards life, while other section of society there are people who are unconcerned about others plight, such selfish and egocentric individuals are motivated to be aggressive towards whoever and whatever is standing in their way, they do not hesitate in destroying lives and livelihood of others.

Structural discrimination and cognitive bias is also responsible for increase in crimes and terrorism, for decades rich industrialized nations governments and officials and super large Multinational companies are or have overwhelmingly focussed on economic growth prospects of two of the world's most populous nations **India and China**, too much emphasis on doing business and investing time and money in India and China, thereby neglecting and ignoring economic growth and business potential that are/were available in abundant in so many other parts and regions of the world.

West-Africa and south-America (Latin-America) are also region rich in natural resources and have considerable large population, yet most large multinational companies have been ignoring these significantly resource rich regions, no major business investments, MNC's only have been taking advantage of available large natural resources in Africa and Latin America to source raw material which are agriculture-commodities and other strategic minerals, for example sourcing agri-commodities like Vanilla and Cocoa-beans from west-Africa and South-American countries in raw form and then using it as raw material to manufacture high-end value added products like Ice-creams, biscuits, chocolates, cakes etc, in factories which are situated in Europe or in India or China and then selling those high-yielding products all over the world, similarly hard-commodities like Iron-ore, bauxite and copper are imported from countries like Australia, Brazil and Chile etc and value added products are manufactured in factories based in China, India and other Asian and European countries.

Advice for resource rich nations, create economic value and don't destroy economic value, *true monetary gains and higher-value is in value addition*, exporting available natural resources in your country in raw form, giving away advantage to others to profit from manufacturing high-value added products, think again, set-up manufacturing facilities in your own country and use available resources as raw material to manufacture value added products, which will give much higher yield and create many challenging opportunities for business and professionals.

There also are other densely populated nations like <u>Bangladesh, Pakistan and Nigeria</u> and also to an extent <u>Philippines and Indonesia</u> are also among countries which haven't attracted large enough business investments, no significant investments in new technology and in manufacturing industries have happen in these countries, thereby notably big majority of population in these countries are deprived of good economic opportunities, unable to find satisfying jobs in their own country many local citizens have to migrate to other countries in search for better career opportunities.

With regards to crimes and criminals as well as terrorists and terrorism, most perpetrated crimes and maximum terrorist activities are centred mainly in west & central Africa and Latin-American countries, maximum percentage of criminal and terrorist activities and spread of dreadful diseases occurs in these regions of the world. Child abuse, war crimes, rape as weapon of war, gang wars, drug trafficking bestial and barbaric crimes are committed in Latin-American and west & central African countries, of course the epicentre of savage Islamic terrorism or the roots of terrorism remains in Pakistan and Afghanistan, the birth place of 21st century terrorism is Afghanistan, the inhuman terrorist groups like <u>Taliban and Al Qaeda</u> are or were formed in Afghanistan,

Because of seriously flawed and corrupt political system no businessmen wants to invest their money in such countries, but, on the flip side, if there are no new business investments happening, no large size industrial projects in their country, all of which adds to more economic pain and therefore rise in poverty, more poverty and more desperation, which compels at least some of the citizens of economically hard-pressed countries to adopt unethical measures, morally unacceptable and violent means to earn money to fight poverty. But also not to ignore another fact, which is that India and China as well have rampant corruption, unpredictable political system and considerably high crime rate.

So majority of population in West & central African countries as well in Latin American countries, and in Egypt, Afghanistan, Bangladesh and Pakistan are desperately poor, living under excruciating situation, with underfunded medical-hospitals and broken medical healthcare system, appalling public and social infrastructure and extreme social backwardness. Among few other reasons it is Poverty the main reason that we've been witnessing and reading a lot about crimes committed in such socioeconomically challenged countries, incidents of crimes like "forced marriages, young girls and women forced into prostitution, sex slavery, human trafficking, drug trafficking and of course terrorism."

But, wait a moment, one pressing question comes in the mind of many of the thoughtful and considerate individual people, if at all, do we have to conclusively believe that poverty is the root cause and sole purpose and reason behind perpetrated crimes and rise in number of criminals and blame poverty for rising terrorism and increasing number of people joining terrorist groups? A tough question to answer, but poverty is only a small factor for rise in crimes around the world, and less to be blame for increasing terrorist activities.

Let us be fair in our assessment, let us not blame poverty stricken poor and less or not educated people for all the social ills. Poor people may not have money but they as well live life with dignity and have self-respect. It is all but true that those of us who take keen interest in global issues and closely observe economic and political affairs have seen and heard of many folks from affluent class committing or found involved in heinous crimes such as Corporate corruption, embezzlement, misappropriation of funds and finances in banking sector, high profile prostitutions, top level bureaucrats and politicians found involve in brazen act of corruption, receiving illegal donations and exploiting various government schemes.

What is more dangerous? And, what is it that is harming humanity the most in 21st century? What this world be like when we enter the 22nd century? These are some of the most pressing questions and concerns, rise in "extremism, terrorism and religious and sectarian conflicts and violence, even more chaotic is > deteriorating natural environment, climatic problems, unpredictable weather," difficult to find quick solutions, it's a fluid situation.

Terrorism, Islamic fundamentalism (jihadi army) or Economic problems, combination of all three factors are responsible for brutally destroying this wonderful Planet of ours **the Earth**. Irresponsibly planned "flawed and faulty economic and international trade policies are having profound and devastating effect and is causing unprecedented harm and damage to natural environment and ecosystem which causes brutal climatic problems," therefore unfounded and irrational beliefs of many that it is terrorism that is menacing and is harming humanity, well, think again, more people around the world are dying or experiencing many types of other excruciating problems all because of more frequent natural disasters.

If we talk and discuss about 21st century challenges, and, what will be the future outlook of global economic and politics? There are political risk, economic risk, deteriorating ecological system, unable to solve ever increasing environmental and climatic problems, all because of growing religious intolerance and sharp increase in incidents of hate crimes. Capitalists economic system "economic policies are planned and implemented to benefit tiny world's population for those who are Rich, influential and power individual people and for the large corporate houses and industries," therefore, small percentage or so to say just 2% of global population is/are immensely benefiting from **Capital-markets** friendly liberal economic policies, but, remaining population of the world is suffering intolerable level of economic hardship, dwindling annual income, higher inflation, ever so rising cost of living, all these factors makes it increasingly difficult for ordinary citizens of the world to sustain themselves and survive.

"Create economic value and do not destroy economic value, higher profits and value is in value addition. Do not give away advantage, learn to make optimal use of the resources you have for your own benefits. Efficient resource management is extremely important to increase productivity, which will immensely help increase profit margins."

It will always be difficult for common people to rightly distinguish between Good or the Bad Evil, so, it is just that odd risk that we have to take in our life of trusting a person or things.

Is life difficult? Yes indeed, this is a greatest truth, but there are people in this world who enjoy hardship, there are people who are not at all scared of difficulty and are confidently ready to meet and accept any and every challenge, then, there are also people who are extremely scared of difficulty and unable to cope with pressure situations, call them cowards if you like, but people who are scared of difficulty such people mostly prefer to stay in comfort zone and to ensure their safety they do not hesitate but are always ready to make ridiculous compromises to keep trouble away from them.

It's normal to feel apprehensive when you try doing something new and different or when you have to face new challenges. Stepping out of the comfort zones and making yourself uncomfortable taking few odd risk can potentially give big rewards. To achieve greater success in life a person needs to initially go through a difficult phase as it is in time of adversity people get great ideas and power to execute those great ideas, which ultimately gives major peace and self-satisfaction when that person gains incredibly higher success in life. So, this is what life is all about, we never know what the end consequences will be of what we intend doing today, it's just that we need to take decisions and make choices of doing things we want to do.

In life, worldwide most people overwhelmingly concentrates mainly on improving their vocabulary and perfecting communication skills, nothing wrong with it, yes, it is always good to have good communication skills and be a good orator, so, what's missing? Well, even more important is, which apparently, sadly, not many people around the world focuses on or bother about, which is developing good **Listening Skills**. Yes, the crux of most problems in the world for the mankind is because most people have rather poor and appalling Listening skills, bad listening characteristic and mannerism of humans can cause and is causing unprecedented and devastating long lasting pain in most us life. Bad listening skills confounds peculiar types of problems and differences of opinion among individuals, leads to arguments and relationships break-ups. The crux of **Domestic Violence** is because people are less attentive among themselves and do not adhere to and listen to each other properly. The effects of domestic violence can destroy professional careers. So, *domestic violence* harms professional as well as sex life.

If there are **problems** there are also **solutions**, no problem or problems are unsolvable, there is/are solution for every problem, but to solve problems you need *courage and determination*, people need to have appropriate knowledge and understanding, this is exactly what lacks in people, there is grave deficit of knowledge and understanding in 99% of our world's population, yes, nearly 99% of world population is/are intellectually incompetent seriously **lacks in "comprehensiveness."** To gain knowledge and to have good ideas, we need to be in habit of getting inspired by all the right things in life, but if you do some research and you'll find majority of people in this world are inspired by all the wrong things, therefore they are less adaptive, people are less productive and more intolerant because they ignore good things and embrace wrong things, people like to read and talk gossip people will waste unprecedented amount of time and money in their life-time reading and discussing gossips and tattling about movie actors and sports personalities, people take keen interest in other people's personal life matters, reads and watch unproductive and meaningless literature and programmes flimsy filmy magazines and cartoon comic books hence such people mind is childish and thought process as good as that of an **infant child**.

Mindless people are unable to **distinguish** between good and bad such people disregards and despise good people who have knowledge and productive ideas, but embrace and respects the wrong people who are corrupt or nitwits, good intelligent people in this world are disrespected and the flawed and faulty people are respected and trusted, people are intolerant because they've no perspective. It is all about *choice you make and decisions you take.*

Difficult people will always create difficult situations, at home or at workplace or for that matter even in social circle, "it will be better not to try and **reason** the **unreasonable** person," so, you need to have the right **temperament** to remain calm in pressure situation.

It is better to walk alone, rather than walk with the crowd who are all walking in wrong direction.

As it is said, that, *you be good to others expect others to be good to you.*

Have a assertive and positive approach, differences and contentious issues needs to be sorted out amicably through dialogue and cordial discussions, one very important lesson to learn in life is, never to **Argue**, *argument is worst form of violence*, arguments normally have devastating consequences, arguments destroys personal image and gives bad reputation, arguments strains relationships or even causes breakup of relationships, be it in personal life, professional or business life, also frequent arguments precipitates domestic violence as well workplace violence, so be better advised, **always avoid argument**.

We can always only listen to person talking and see his/her expression and body language, but, what we can't do is, that, we can't access the other persons thoughts, hence the person/persons we deal with, we have to just look at and take things at face value, it will always be impossible for us to understand as to what is it that's really going on in his/her mind.

Different individuals have different Perception and Conviction; Our Perceptions and Convictions are self-serving purpose for our betterment, but our perceptions and convictions at times proves to be self-defeating, more often than not our worse enemy can't harm us as much we harm our own-selves, it is just because some individuals don't learn to accept their mistakes and take blame for their misfortune on themselves, people have tendency of blaming others for their plight.

Don't downgrade your dreams just to fit your reality, upgrade your conviction to make your destiny.

Maturity is not when we start thinking big things, it is when we start understanding small things.

Sometimes it is better to be kind than to be right. We do not need an intelligent mind that speaks, but a patient heart that listens.

If Mistakes have been Committed, so, Learn from the Past Mistakes and Have it Correct the Next time.